THE BOY ALLIES IN GREAT PERIL

Or, With the Italian Army in the Alps

CLAIR W. HAYES

1st WORLD
LIBRARY
Literary Society

The Boy Allies in Great Peril

Clair W. Hayes

© 1st World Library, 2009
PO Box 2211
Fairfield, IA 52556
www.1stworldlibrary.com
First Edition

LCCN: 2009923372

Softcover ISBN: 978-1-4218-8820-0
Hardcover ISBN: 978-1-4218-8919-1
eBook ISBN: 978-1-4218-8721-0

Purchase *"The Boy Allies in Great Peril"*
as a traditional bound book at:
www.1stWorldLibrary.com/purchase.asp?ISBN=978-1-4218-8820-0

1st World Library is a literary, educational organization
dedicated to:

- Creating a free internet library of downloadable ebooks

- Hosting writing competitions and offering book publishing
  scholarships.

Interested in more 1st World Library books? contact:
literacy@1stworldlibrary.com
Check us out at: www.1stworldlibrary.com

1st World Library Literary Society

Giving Back to the World

"If you want to work on the core problem, it's early school literacy."

- James Barksdale, former CEO of Netscape

"No skill is more crucial to the future of a child, or to a democratic and prosperous society, than literacy."

- Los Angeles Times

"Literacy... means far more than learning how to read and write... The aim is to transmit... knowledge and promote social participation."

- UNESCO

"Literacy is not a luxury, it is a right and a responsibility. If our world is to meet the challenges of the twenty-first century we must harness the energy and creativity of all our citizens."

- President Bill Clinton

"Parents should be encouraged to read to their children, and teachers should be equipped with all available techniques for teaching literacy, so the varying needs and capacities of individual kids can be taken into account."

- Hugh Mackay

CHAPTER I

THE BREWING STORM

"Did you ever see such a mob, Hal?"

The speaker was an American lad of some seventeen years of age. He stopped in his walk as he spoke and grasped his companion by the arm. The latter allowed his gaze to rove over the thousands upon thousands of people who thronged the approach to the king's palace at Rome, before he replied:

"Some mob, Chester; some mob."

"Looks like a real army could be recruited from this bunch," continued the first speaker.

"Rather," agreed the other. "And unless I am mightily mistaken that is what will be done. Most of them are soldiers anyhow, you know."

"True. I had forgotten we were in Italy, where military service is compulsory. Then you think that Italy has at last decided to enter the war?"

"I certainly do. The Chamber of Deputies has done its best to keep Italy from becoming involved, but the voice of the people must be heeded sooner or later. I believe the time has come."

"I am sure I hope so," said Chester. "Italy's army, entirely ready for any eventuality, should turn the balance in favor of the Allies."

"And I believe it will," said Hal.

"Do you believe the announcement of a state of war between Italy and Austria will be formally made to-day?"

"I do—and so, apparently, do the others here," and Hal swept his arm about him in a comprehensive gesture. "Hear them shout!"

For a mighty cheer had suddenly risen upon the air. Wildly excited Italians—men and women from all walks of life— seemed to have gone suddenly mad. A deafening roar filled the air. Caps and hats, canes, and other articles ascended and descended in a dense cloud.

"Can you doubt, after that, that Italy is for war?" asked Hal, when at last he could make himself heard.

"I guess not," replied Chester grimly. "But why should the crowd have gathered in front of the palace rather than before the Chamber of Deputies?"

"You forget that the premier is closeted with the king," returned Hal. "In all probability, the first word of a definite step will emanate from the palace, though unofficially, of course."

"I see," said Chester. "Well—look there, Hal!"

"What's the matter?" demanded the latter, eying his companion in some surprise.

Chester seized his friend's arm with one hand and with the other pointed directly ahead. Hal gazed in the direction indicated. He saw at once what had caused Chester's sudden exclamation.

Not five yards away, right in the center of the dense crowd, but still in view of the two boys, stood an Italian army officer in full uniform. He was gazing straight ahead toward the palace steps, paying no heed to those who pushed and jostled him. He stood erect, with arms folded upon his breast.

Even as the two boys looked, an arm came from behind him, and reaching across his shoulder, a hand crept cautiously into the pocket of the officer's military cloak, which he had thrown open because of its warmth.

Hal uttered a low exclamation and was about to step forward when there came a sudden shout from the crowd, which surged in about him, cutting off his view of the Italian officer. For a single instant Hal turned his eyes toward the palace and there took one look at a second uniformed figure, who stood upon the top step and waved his arms about violently.

"I guess war has come," the boy muttered to himself, as he took a step forward and elbowed his way toward the spot where the other Italian officer stood.

Chester came close behind his friend.

By dint of hard pushing and shoving, which drew ugly remarks from some of the bystanders upon whose feet they trod, the boys at last came to the spot they sought. They had made good time and the invisible owner of the hand that had explored the officer's pocket was just withdrawing it. And in it Hal saw a white paper flutter.

He uttered a cry and dashed forward in spite of the crowd. At almost the same moment the officer came to life. Instinct must have warned him that there was something wrong. He clapped his hand to his pocket, and then uttered a fierce ejaculation in his native tongue.

He wheeled about with a cry, and his arm shot out. There was a struggle, and then the officer fell to the ground. A blow from his adversary's fist had laid him low. Hal, who was a few leaps ahead of Chester, reached out to seize the man, who, he could see, still held the bit of white paper in his hand, but the other was too quick for him.

With a sudden backward leap he was among the crowd, which, apparently, had failed to grasp the significance of the trouble. Hal uttered a quick cry to Chester and also dashed into the crowd. Chester followed him.

Ahead, but almost hidden by others of the crowd, which pressed forward the better to see what was going on upon the palace steps, Hal could see his quarry squirming his way through the dense mass of humanity.

"Stop him!" he cried, raising his voice to a shout.

The crowd paid no heed. The people were too wrapped up in what was going on before the palace to notice the three who were trying to force their way through. Again Hal cried out, but the result was the same.

For a brief instant the fugitive glanced over his shoulder, and he waved a hand at Hal. It was the first time the lad had seen

Clair W. Hayes

his face, and he knew that he would recognize it again wherever he saw it.

"I'll get you yet," declared Hal to himself between tightly shut lips. "I'll get you if it takes a year."

He pressed on, with Chester close at his heels.

Turning and squirming and twisting their way, the lads managed to plod on through the dense crowd at a snail's pace. Ahead of them, however, Hal could see that the fugitive was making about the same progress. His hopes rose, and he called over his shoulder to Chester;

"Keep coming; we'll get him!"

Chester made no reply, for he knew none was expected. He kept close behind his friend.

Now, suddenly, the fugitive reached the edge of the crowd. For a single moment he paused, and gazed back at his pursuers. Once more he waved a hand at Hal, and then, turning, started off at a run.

Hal, seeing that his quarry was about to make good his escape, suddenly grew angry. Bringing some tactics learned on the football field into play, he dashed forward, hurling spectators to right and left. In another moment he, too, had reached the edge of the crowd and, with a cry, dashed ahead.

He did not pause to see whether Chester was behind him. All he thought of was to overtake the fugitive.

Chester, in attempting to follow his friend, stumbled over an outstretched foot and fell heavily to the ground. He was not badly hurt, but he had struck on his face and for a moment he was dazed. He dragged himself quickly to his feet and moved forward again. Some distance ahead he saw that Hal was gaining upon the fugitive.

Down the wide street ran the fugitive, with Hal close behind and gaining at every stride. As the sound of pursuing footsteps became plainer, the man looked back over his shoulder. Then he redoubled his efforts; but still Hal gained.

Suddenly the man dashed around a corner. Three seconds later Hal did the same. As he did so he caught sight of a big man before him. Hal tried to check his pace, but it was too late.

Something bright flashed in the sunlight and Hal felt a sickening thud upon his head. In vain he tried to keep his feet. He sank slowly to the ground and then fell forward on his face. And even as he lost consciousness, he thought to himself:

"What a fool I was. I should have suspected a trap. So he hit me with the butt of a revolver. I'll get even yet."

Above the fallen lad the man stood with a grim smile of satisfaction. He stirred the prostrate form with his foot and then put his revolver back in his pocket. He turned to go.

At that moment Chester dashed around the corner. The lad and the fugitive took in the situation at the same moment. Chester pulled himself up short and reached for his revolver, which he always carried in his coat pocket. But the other was too quick for him. He leaped suddenly forward and Chester's arm was seized in a vise-like grip.

In vain the lad struggled to free himself. He could not move the powerful fingers that gripped him. He kicked out with his

Clair W. Hayes

right foot and this effort was rewarded by a cry of pain from his opponent.

"Kick me on the shins, will you?" cried the latter in German.

His free hand found the revolver in his pocket and it flashed in the sunlight once more. He attempted to reverse the weapon and seize it by the barrel, and as he did so he unconsciously loosened his grip upon Chester's arm.

The latter swung himself about suddenly and with a sweep of his arm sent the man's revolver clattering to the ground. The other uttered an exclamation of rage, and stepped back.

Chester again reached for his own revolver, but once more the other was too quick for him. He came forward with a jump, and his right fist shot out. Chester ducked this blow, but he was unprepared for the left-handed blow that followed.

As he came up after ducking the first blow, the second caught him squarely upon the point of the chin, and he toppled over. It was a clean knockout.

"I guess that will settle you," said the victor, as he surveyed the prostrate forms of his two enemies. "I guess that will teach you not to interfere in other people's business. Hello, one of them is moving."

He gazed curiously at Hal, who at that moment opened his eyes. The man stood undecided a moment. Then he took a step toward the boy, but stopped again.

"No," he muttered. "What's the use? Let him be."

He swung upon his heel and made his way down the street. A moment later he was lost to sight around a corner.

CHAPTER II

THE TWO FRIENDS

While Hal and Chester are still upon the ground and consciousness is gradually returning, it will be well to introduce a few words concerning them, that those who have not made their acquaintance before may learn just what sort of boys our heroes are.

Hal Paine and Chester Crawford were typical American boys. With the former's mother, they had been in Berlin when the great European conflagration broke out and had been stranded there. Mrs. Paine had been able to get out of the country, but Hal and Chester were left behind.

In company with Major Raoul Derevaux, a Frenchman, and Captain Harry Anderson, an Englishman, they finally made their way into Belgium, where they arrived in time to take part in the heroic defense of Liége in the early stages of the war. Here they rendered such invaluable service to the Belgian commander that they were commissioned lieutenants in the little army of King Albert.

Both in fighting and in scouting they had proven their worth. Following the first Belgian campaign, the two lads had seen service with the British troops on the continent, where they

Clair W. Hayes

were attached to the staff of General Sir John French, in command of the English forces. Also they had won the respect and admiration of General Joffre, the French commander-in-chief.

As related in the third book of this series, "The Boy Allies with the Cossacks," Hal and Chester had seen active service under the Russian Bear in the eastern theater of war. They fought in the midst of the Russian forces and were among the troop of 60,000 that made the first wild dash over the Carpathians to the plains of Hungary.

Returning to the western war area with despatches from the Grand Duke Nicholas to the French commander-in-chief, they had again taken up their duties with the British army. As related in "The Boy Allies in the Trenches," they had been instrumental in defeating more than one German coup, and it was through them, also, that a plot to assassinate President Poincaré had failed.

Both lads were about the same age. Large and strong, they were proficient in the use of their fists and of the art of swordsmanship, and were entirely familiar with firearms. Another thing that stood them in good stead was the fact that both spoke French and German fluently. Also, each had a smattering of Italian.

Following their coup in saving the French president from the hands of traitorous Apaches in Paris, Hal and Chester had come to Rome with their mothers, whom they had found in Paris, and Chester's uncle. They had not come without protest, for both had been eager to get back to the firing line, but their mothers' entreaties had finally prevailed. As Chester's Uncle John had said, "This is none of our war. Your place, boys, is with your mothers."

Chester and Hal had sought consent to rejoin the army in vain. Neither Mrs. Paine nor Mrs. Crawford would hear of such a thing. So at last they agreed to return home. First, however, at Uncle John's suggestion, the party decided to stop in Rome.

"Italy is still a sane and peaceable country," Uncle John had said.

Naturally the lads had been greatly interested in the war demonstrations in Rome. Uncle John, who at first had "pooh-poohed" the prospect of Italy's entering the war, finally had been convinced that such a course was only a matter of time. Mrs. Paine and Mrs. Crawford, realizing how greatly interested their sons were becoming, immediately decided to return to America. They feared that some harm would come to Hal and Chester—feared that the boys might be drawn into trouble again—for they both knew their dispositions not to shirk danger.

The war situation at this time was anything but favorable to the Allies. Along the great western battle line, stretching out from the North Sea far to the south, the mighty armies were gripped in a deadlock. Occasional advances would be made by both sides and retreats would follow.

Having pushed the invader back from the very walls of Paris soon after the outbreak of hostilities, the French had shoved him across the Aisne and then across the Marne. But here the allied offensive halted. Grand assaults and heroic charges proved ineffectual. The Kaiser's troops were strongly intern-ched and could not be dislodged. On their side, the Allies' positions were equally impregnable and repeated assaults by the enemy had failed to shake their lines.

In the eastern theater of war the Russians, at this moment,

were meeting with some success. Several large Austrian strongholds had been captured after the bloodiest fighting of the war, and it was believed that it would only be a question of a few weeks until the Russian Grand Duke would develop his long-expected invasion of Hungary.

In the north of the eastern war arena, also, the Russians had met with some success, Poland had been invaded, and around Warsaw the great German drive had been checked. The sea was still free of German ships, with the exception of the submarines which still continued to prey upon all commerce, neutral as well as Allies'.

The situation in the Balkan states remained unchanged. It was hoped that the Balkan countries would rally to the support of the Allies, and thus form an iron ring about the Germanic powers, but this matter was no nearer a successful issue than it had been months before. However, diplomats of both sides were still busy in the Balkans, and each hoped to gain their support.

But for the last few weeks all eyes had been turned toward Italy. A member of the Austro-German Triple Alliance at the beginning of the war, Italy had refused to support a war of aggression by the Kaiser and had severed her connection with the Alliance. She had announced that she would remain neutral.

At length, however, matters reached such a pass that Italy realized she must cast her lot with the Allies. She knew that should the Germans emerge from the war victorious she had all to lose and nothing to gain. The first act of the successful German army would be to crush her. Besides, there had always been antagonism between Austria and Italy, and the drawing of Italy into the Triple Alliance in the first place was considered an act of trickery. Austria and Italy could have nothing in common.

The people of Italy demanded that she throw her military as well as her moral support to the Allies. The matter had been threshed out in the Chamber of Deputies. Wild anti-German and anti-Austrian demonstrations were almost daily occurrences in the streets of Rome and other of the larger Italian cities. The people wanted war. Here was the one country of all the powers engaged in the mighty conflict that could truthfully say: "This is a popular war."

At the instigation of the Kaiser, Austria had agreed to make many concessions to Italy in return for her neutrality. She agreed to almost anything. But the Italian government was not fooled. Austria would yield anything at the present time, and then, with the aid of her powerful ally, Germany, at the close of the war, take it away from Italy again.

So the Italian people and the Italian government decided upon war on the side of the Allies. Millions of trained fighting men, fresh from the rigors of the recent Turkish war, were ready to take the field at almost a moment's notice. The reserves had already been ordered to the colors. The Italian fleet was ready for action.

There was now no question that Italy would enter the war. The chief topic of interest was as to where she would strike first. Would she send an army to join the French and British troops recently landed on the Gallipoli peninsula and a portion of her fleet to help force the Dardanelles, or would she strike first at Austria, and if so, would the first blow be delivered by her fleet in the Adriatic, or to the north, upon the border, and through the Alps?

The Chamber of Deputies had been in continuous session now for almost two days. It was known that upon the result of this conference hinged the issue, peace or war. The chamber was still in session, but the Premier had left and sought King Victor Emmanuel at the palace for a consultation.

News of this kind travels quickly. The great mob which had assembled outside the Chamber of Deputies wended its way to the palace, where it stood awaiting some word of what action was to be taken. The people knew that the answer would not be long coming.

Hal Paine and Chester Crawford were standing in the midst of this crowd when this story opens. They had just left their mothers and Uncle John at their hotel, announcing that they would get the latest war news. The two women had offered no objection, but Uncle John had instructed them:

"Don't be gone long, boys. Remember we leave in the morning, and we expect you to do your share of the packing."

So the two lads had strolled out and joined the crowd.

When they had decided to return to America, each lad had carefully packed his British uniform, so they were now in civilian clothes. This was a matter of some regret to them, for they had been proud of their uniforms, and not without cause, and even as they walked along to-day Chester had remarked:

"We should have our uniforms on, Hal."

"Why?" demanded the latter.

"Well, just look at all these Italian officers. It makes me feel lonesome to be without my uniform."

Hal laughed.

"By Jove! it does at that," he agreed. "I can sympathize with the soldier who has such an absolute disgust for a civilian. You know there is no love lost between them."

"Right! Well, I wish I had my uniform on."

"It's a good thing you haven't, I guess. That warlike spirit of yours might get us in trouble. Every time I look at mine, I want to run back to the front instead of going home."

"It is pretty tough," agreed Chester.

"You bet it is. But what else could we do? We must please our mothers, you know."

"I suppose you're right. But just the same, several times I have had a notion to disappear."

"The same thought struck me, too; but we gave our promise, you know."

Chester shrugged his shoulders.

"It can't be helped now," he said.

"Maybe we'll have a little war of our own some day," said Hal. "Then they'll have to let us fight."

"That would be too good to be true," was Chester's reply.

It was just at the end of this conversation that the lads had joined the crowd before the palace, and Chester had made the remark that opens this story.

CHAPTER III

THE MOB

Hal sat up and passed his right hand gently over his head.

"Quite a bump," he muttered to himself. "What a fool I was not to have been prepared for that ruse. Well, I'll know better next time."

The lad pulled himself to his feet and gazed in the direction in which the other had disappeared. He made as if to move after him, and then changed his mind.

"Not much chance of finding him now, I guess," he muttered.

He turned on his heel, and then, for the first time, his eyes fell upon Chester's prostrate form.

"So he got you, too, eh?" he said to himself.

He hurried forward and bent over his chum. At the same moment Chester opened his eyes and smiled up at him feebly.

"Hello," he said; "where's our friend?"

"Gone," replied Hal briefly, raising Chester's head to his knee. "How do you feel?"

"A little rocky, and that's a fact," was the reply.

"What did he bump you over with—gun?"

"No; fist."

"I don't see any marks."

"I feel 'em," said Chester, rubbing his chin ruefully. "He landed an uppercut that was a beauty."

"I am glad you are well enough to appreciate it," said Hal, with a slight smile. "He was big enough to have put you out for keeps."

"I'm not to be gotten rid of so easily," returned Chester. "Help me up."

Hal lent a supporting hand and Chester struggled to his feet.

"Dizzy?" queried Hal.

"A little," was the reply. "I'll be all right in a minute, though."

He shook his head several times and at last appeared to have gotten rid of the effects of the blow. He threw off Hal's hand.

"Well, what now?" he asked.

Hal hesitated.

"I hate to see that fellow get away," he said finally. "He

probably has stolen important information."

"I guess there is not much doubt of that," replied Chester, "but Rome is a pretty sizeable town. A slim chance we have of finding him."

"I'd know him if I see him," said Hal

"So will I. Did you notice the scar across his face?"

"Yes; that's why I say I would know him any place. What do you suppose it was he stole?"

"A paper of some kind; I saw that. Probably has to do with troop movements or something of the sort. You remember he stole it from an army officer."

"Yes; which reminds me that he also disposed of said army officer without much trouble. The last I saw of him he was floundering about on the ground in the midst of the crowd."

"Let's go back and have a look for him."

"Good; come on."

The boys turned and retraced their steps. Rounding a corner they came again within sight of the palace.

"Crowd still there," Hal commented briefly.

It was true. The crowd seemed to have grown rather than to have diminished.

"Something must have happened while we were gone," said Chester. "Hear them yell."

"I guess it means war," was Hal's quiet response. "Well, I'm glad."

"And so am I. This German business should be settled without much trouble now."

"Don't you believe it. The Kaiser is good for a long, hard fight yet."

They pushed their way through the crowd. Suddenly they came to a stop, their further progress being barred by a solid mass of humanity directly in front of them, Hal took Chester by the arm.

"Let's see what is going on here," he said.

By dint of hard pushing and shoving they worked their way gradually through the crowd.

"As I live, it's our friend the army officer," ejaculated Hal.

"So it is," agreed Chester, "and he seems to be rather excited. Look at him waving his arms about."

Surrounded by a curious crowd, the officer referred to was declaiming eloquently. It was plain from the attitude of the crowd, however, that he wasn't making himself plain.

"He's too excited to talk coherently," said Hal. "Maybe we can help him out a bit. Let's get through the rest of this gang."

He put his elbows in front of him, and closely followed by Chester, threw his weight upon the mass of humanity in front. The crowd parted, and the lads pushed their way through, unheeding the protests their rough methods called forth. They stopped beside the still excited officer.

"Signor—" began Hal, but the officer paid no attention to him, and continued to wave his arms violently about.

"You can't get his attention that way," said Chester. "Let me try."

He grasped the Italian officer roughly by the arm and whirled him about.

Immediately the latter's arms ceased their violent gesticulations and he turned an angry face upon Chester.

"How dare you lay your hands upon an officer of the king?" he demanded in a harsh voice.

His hand dropped to his holster.

"Here! Here!" exclaimed Hal. "Hold your horses now and don't get excited. We've come to tell you something about that paper you lost."

"Ah!" cried the Italian. "So you have it, eh? Give it to me!"

He held out a hand expectantly.

"No, we haven't it," replied Hal, "but—"

"Give me the paper!" cried the officer, his voice becoming shrill with anger.

"I tell you we haven't the paper," said Hal.

"That's a lie!" shouted the Italian. "You knocked me down and stole the paper."

He clutched Hal by the arm.

"Let go of me," said the lad angrily. "We are trying to help you and—"

The Italian officer now suddenly drew his revolver, and pointed it squarely at Hal.

"Give me the paper or I shall shoot," he said more quietly.

He staggered suddenly backward and the revolver dropped to the ground with a clatter. The Italian wheeled and confronted the angry face of Chester, who had struck up the weapon.

"What's the matter with you? Can't you see we are trying to help you?" demanded Chester.

At this point there came a diversion. Members of the crowd who had witnessed the dispute between the officer and the two lads suddenly set up a cry of "spies."

Others behind them took it up.

"Spies! Spies!" a hundred voices rang out.

The crowd surged in about them.

Hal gave one quick look about, and then said quietly to Chester:

"We are in for it now, old man. We'll have to make a break for it."

"All right," said Chester grimly. "Lead the way."

Once more the Italian officer stretched forth a detaining

hand, but this time Hal wasted no time in explanation. He struck out straight from the shoulder, and the officer toppled to the ground.

"Second fall for him to-day," muttered Hal between his teeth.

He felt Chester's arm press his elbow.

"Come on," he said.

Side by side the lads stepped forward in the very faces of the mob that barred their path, and for a moment the crowd gave back. Then one man, bolder than the rest, sprang forward and sought to clutch Chester's arm. The lad's fist met him half way and he dropped silently to the ground.

An angry roar went up from the crowd.

Chester's hand dropped to his pocket. Hal perceived the motion and cried out:

"No guns, Chester!"

Chester realized the soundness of the warning and his revolver remained where it was.

Two of the crowd sprang forward together, but Hal and Chester, with their greater strength and reach, disposed of them easily. A blow from behind landed on Chester's neck and he staggered forward. He recovered himself in a moment, however, and shouted.

"Rush 'em, Hal!"

The latter also realized that to stand still and fight gave the crowd behind too great an opening and he obeyed Chester's injunction. At the same moment both sprang forward, and the crowd opened before them.

Straight ahead they went, striking out right and left, but rushing forward as fast as possible all the time. Men fell on both sides of them beneath their heavy blows, and so far neither lad had received a severe jolt.

At that moment, however, Hal felt a keen pain in his left arm. He glanced down curiously and saw a tiny stream of red spout forth. His lips set in a thin line.

"Guns, Chester," he said quietly, halting in his tracks. "They are using knives."

"Good," said Chester, also halting. "Back to back."

The lads whipped out their automatics simultaneously, and, back to back, confronted the crowd. Hal spoke.

"We are not spies," he shouted, "but we are not going to be killed without a fight. We are British army officers. Stand back!"

Before the threatening muzzles of the two automatics the crowd hesitated. Then, from directly ahead of Chester, a shot rang out. The lad heard something whiz past his head, and from beyond came a cry of pain.

"Shot one of his own number," muttered the lad.

His finger tightened on the trigger as he saw a man about to leap forward regardless of the automatic.

"I'm going to shoot, Hal," he called.

"I guess it can't be helped," replied the lad quietly. "When I give the word turn loose on 'em, and then we'll make another break."

He hesitated a single instant and then called:

"Ready?"

"Ready!" came the reply.

"Then—" began Hal, and suddenly cried, "Wait!"

For at that moment the crowd in front of him suddenly began to scatter, and from beyond Hal made out a troop of Italian cavalry bearing down on them with drawn sabers. Hal lowered his weapon and called out:

"It's all right, Chester!"

CHAPTER IV

AN OLD FRIEND

"What's the meaning of this?" demanded an officer, pulling in his horse beside the two lads, while his troop gave their attention to driving back the crowd, which gave ground slowly.

"We were attacked by the crowd, captain," Hal explained.

"Why?" asked the officer.

"We were accused of being spies."

"By whom?"

"By an Italian army officer back there," replied Hal, making a gesture with his hand.

"Here he comes now," interrupted Chester.

The man who had caused all the trouble now came pompously forward. At sight of him, the mounted officer sprang from the saddle and came to attention.

"What is the matter, sir?" he asked.

Clair W. Hayes

"Arrest these two," said his superior, pointing to Hal and Chester. "They are spies, and they knocked me down."

The Italian captain motioned to half a dozen of his men. He also pointed to the two lads.

"Arrest them," he said quietly.

The men surrounded the lads.

"But—" began Chester.

"No words," said the officer. "Take them before General Ferrari," he ordered his men.

He motioned to the commander of the troop to accompany them.

"I shall be there to make the charge against them," he said.

The young officer saluted.

"Very well, sir," he replied. He turned to the lads. "March," he ordered.

There was no help for it, as the lads realized in a moment. Accordingly they made no further protests and marched off, surrounded on all sides.

As they walked along the street there came a new diversion. A man came hurrying toward them. Hal and Chester recognized him in an instant.

"Uncle John!" cried Chester.

He glanced at Hal and smiled sheepishly.

"We seem always to be in trouble when he appears," said Chester with a slight smile.

Uncle John addressed the officer in command of the squad.

"What's the meaning of this?" he demanded.

"The meaning of what, sir?" asked the officer respectfully, for he was impressed by Uncle John's manner.

"What are you doing with these two lads?"

"They are under arrest, sir."

"What!" ejaculated Uncle John. "Under arrest, and what for?"

"They are spies."

"Spies!" The good man staggered back. He forced a smile. "You are joking with me," he said.

The Italian officer drew himself up.

"I never joke of serious matters," he said quietly. "But what interest have you in these prisoners?"

"Well, I have considerable interest," was the reply. "One of them happens to be my nephew. What have they been doing?"

"I couldn't say as to that. All I know is that they are spies."

"You're crazy," shouted Uncle John, now becoming angry. "They are British army officers, and American citizens."

The young officer drew himself up.

"Crazy, am I?" he demanded. "March!" he ordered his men.

"Here, hold on a minute," gasped Uncle John. "I didn't mean to ruffle your feelings; but one of those boys is my nephew. I tell you they are British officers."

"I trust they will be able to prove it," said the Italian.

"What?" demanded Uncle John. "Why?"

"Because," replied the officer with a pleasant smile, "they probably will be shot if they don't."

"Shot!" gasped Uncle John.

"Exactly. That is the usual treatment accorded spies."

"But I tell you—"

"You can tell the rest to General Ferrari," said the Italian officer. "Forward, men."

Uncle John was brushed unceremoniously aside in spite of his protests, and the lads were led away.

"Don't worry, Uncle John," Chester called back to him. "We'll get out of this all right. Tell mother to have no fear."

"I'll see the ambassador!" shouted Uncle John. "I'll get you out of this. I'll show these confounded Italians they are not half as big as Uncle Sam."

"Poor old Uncle John," said Chester to Hal. "He does get excited so easily. I'll bet the ambassador is due for an unpleasant half hour."

"I'd give a whole lot to be there to hear what transpires," agreed Hal.

In front of a large and imposing building the Italian officer called a halt; and a few minutes later ordered the prisoners up the steps.

"Where are we going?" demanded Hal.

"You'll find out soon enough," was the reply.

"You're very civil and courteous, to be sure," said Hal.

"I can see no reason for being courteous to a spy," replied the officer.

"Perhaps not," returned the lad; "but when we are out of this I believe I shall hunt you up and pull your nose."

"What!" exclaimed the officer, stepping back. "Pull my nose! Such American impudence! I have a notion to pull your nose right here."

"I wouldn't if I were you," said Chester, grinning.

"And what have you to say about it?" exclaimed the now angry officer.

"Oh, nothing," replied Chester. "Just a kindly word of warning; that's all."

The officer stared at both lads angrily, as they stood at the top of the steps, and seemed about to say more, when a second officer appeared in the doorway and motioned for all to enter.

"Move on there," said the first officer angrily.

The lads obeyed without replying.

Inside the building they were led through a long corridor, and thence to a room which they were motioned to enter. Inside stood a tall, stout man attired in full military uniform.

"General Ferrari, I guess," Chester whispered to his friend.

Hal nodded in assent. It was indeed General Ferrari, and he came forward.

"What have we here?" he demanded, addressing the officer.

"Spies, sir," was the reply.

"Where did you find them?"

The officer explained.

"So Colonel Fuesco found them, eh? You say they stole an important document from him?"

"Yes, sir, and the colonel will be here directly, sir."

"Good, you may go. Leave a guard outside the door."

The officer saluted and took his departure, casting a sneering glance at the two lads.

"Sit down," commanded the general.

The lads obeyed, and the general took a seat at a huge desk at the far end of the room and immediately plunged into a mass of correspondence. For half an hour he was busy with his letters and paid no attention to the boys. The latter also sat silently.

An orderly entered the room and announced:

"Colonel Fuesco, sir."

"Show him in," said the general.

A moment later and the colonel came blustering in. He gazed angrily at the two lads and spoke to General Ferrari in a whisper. Then both turned upon the lads.

"Have you the paper?" demanded the general.

"No, sir," replied Hal. "We never had it in the first place. Will you allow me to explain, sir?"

"Proceed," said the general.

"First," said Hal, "I would inform your excellency that we are officers in the British army, having recently come from France."

He then went ahead with the story of how they had seen Colonel Fuesco relieved of his papers before the palace a short time ago. At the conclusion of the story the colonel sniffed audibly.

"A likely tale," he sneered.

"Silence, colonel," said the general sharply. "I shall go at this matter in my own way. Can you prove your identity?" he

Clair W. Hayes

asked of Hal.

"With time, yes," was the reply.

At this moment the orderly again entered the room.

"The officer you were expecting, sir," he said to General Ferrari.

"Have him enter," said the general, and the orderly saluted and disappeared.

"There can be no doubt that these are spies, sir," said Colonel Fuesco.

Chester became suddenly angry.

"That's a lie," he said flatly.

"What!" exclaimed the doughty colonel. "You call me a liar?"

Before General Ferrari or Hal could move to stay him, he stepped close to Chester and struck him in the face.

Hal, knowing Chester's quick temper, became alarmed and cried out sharply:

"Don't hit him, Chester."

But he spoke too late. The blow aroused Chester's fighting blood and he took no thought of consequences. His right fist shot out sharply, and struck squarely upon the nose, the colonel reeled back and fell to the floor.

He was up in a moment, however, and in spite of his

commander's sharp order, closed with Chester. The two rocked back and forth, as Hal and General Ferrari sought to separate them.

And at this moment a newcomer entered the room. He was a young man, thin and tall, and his face showed the marks of hard service. He was attired in the uniform of a French major. He, too, took a hand in attempting to separate the combatants.

As the five struggled about, Hal caught a glimpse of the newcomer's face, and he gave a cry of wonder, uttering a name that caused Chester to release his hold upon the Italian officer and step back in surprise and pleasure.

"Major Derevaux!" exclaimed Hal.

Clair W. Hayes

CHAPTER V

A NEW RECRUIT

The French officer also stepped back in surprise, for until that moment he had not had time to glance at the two lads. He, too, gave vent to an exclamation of pleasure and held out both hands.

"Hal! Chester!" he cried.

Each lad seized upon a hand and wrung it heartily. General Ferrari and Colonel Fuesco stood back and eyed them curiously. Finally the general spoke to the Frenchman.

"You know these boys?" he asked.

"Know them!" repeated Major Derevaux. "Well, I should say I do. They are Lieutenants Paine and Crawford, of His British majesty's service, sir."

"Then they are not German or Austrian spies?"

"What! These lads German spies! If you but knew of what invaluable service they have been to the cause of the Allies, you would be proud to shake hands with them. Why, let me tell you," and forgetting all other matters for the moment,

Major Derevaux plunged into an account of the boys' triumphs since joining the allied forces.

At the conclusion of this recital, General Ferrari extended a hand to each of the boys.

"I am indeed glad to know two such gallant lads," he said. "I felt sure when I first saw you that there must be some mistake in your cases."

"But they stole my paper!" cried Colonel Fuesco.

"That is not true," said Major Derevaux. "I can vouch for their loyalty."

"But who can vouch for you?" demanded the colonel. "How is General Ferrari to know that you, too, are not a spy, coming to him with false credentials?"

"I can answer that question," replied the general. "As it happens, I have known Major Derevaux for years. He has often visited at my home, he and his parents. You owe these lads an apology, colonel."

"He knocked me down," replied the colonel, pointing to Chester.

"So he did," said the general, "and you deserved it."

Chester now approached the colonel and extended a hand.

"I bear you no ill will," he said.

The officer glanced at him searchingly for a moment, and then took the hand.

"I have done you and your friend an injustice," he said. "I am sorry."

"Say no more about it," replied Chester.

Colonel Fuesco also shook hands with Hal.

"But what of my paper?" he demanded of the general.

"I can give you a description of the man who took it," said Hal, and did so. When he mentioned that the man had a scar on his face, the two Italian officers uttered a cry.

"Hans Robard!" they exclaimed.

"You know him, then?" asked Chester.

"Rather," said the general dryly. "He is an Austrian, and attached to the Austrian embassy here. Of course there has as yet been no formal declaration of war between Italy and Austria, but it has been known for days that war was sure to come. Colonel Fuesco here has been entrusted with important documents relating to troop movements, and it is this document that Robard has stolen. It must be recovered."

"We are willing to help all we can," said Chester. "With a little forethought we should have been able to recover it ourselves. Robard made monkeys of us."

"He made a monkey of me, too," said the colonel ruefully.

"The thing to be done," said Chester, "is to get track of him."

"That's easy enough," was the reply. "He can be found at the embassy; but he will deny that he has the paper. Also, we cannot arrest him. Being a member of a foreign embassy, in times of peace he is immune from arrest."

"And he will take the paper with him when he leaves Italy," said Major Derevaux.

"It was stolen once," said Hal thoughtfully. "Why cannot it be stolen again?"

"What do you mean?" asked Colonel Fuesco.

"Just what I say. Robard stole the document from you. Some one must recover it from Robard without his knowledge."

"An excellent idea!" exclaimed General Ferrari. "But who will do this work?"

"We shall be glad to undertake it, your excellency," said Hal.

"You! But you are so young for such a piece of work."

"Don't you believe it, general," Major Derevaux interrupted. "If the papers can be recovered, these lads can get them. You could not put the mission in better hands."

"But the danger—"

"We have been in danger before, sir," said Chester quietly.

The general considered a moment, and then brought a hand down on his desk with tremendous force.

"So be it!" he exclaimed. "And if you are successful, Italy will know how to reward you."

"We seek no reward, sir," said Hal quietly. "Then we are at liberty to go now, sir?"

Clair W. Hayes

"Yes. I shall not hamper you with instructions."

"All we wish to know, sir," said Hal, "is whether Robard still is at the Austrian embassy."

"He is," was the reply, "and will be until some time to-morrow, when the ambassador will be given his passports."

"Can I be of any assistance?" asked Colonel Fuesco, stepping forward.

"If you can, we shall call on you," replied Hal.

"Good," said the colonel, and, drawing out a card, he scribbled an address on it. "You will find me there," he said. "I shall remain at my quarters in the hopes that I may be given a hand in the game."

The lads shook hands with the general and walked to the door.

"Wait a moment, boys," said Major Derevaux. "I want a few words with the general, and then I shall be at liberty to go with you."

"If it is all the same to you, Major Derevaux," said the general, "I would prefer to postpone our conference until this evening. I have several matters that require my immediate attention."

Major Derevaux accepted this postponement graciously, and announced that he would accompany the boys at once. As they would have passed out, the general's orderly once more entered the room.

"The American ambassador is without, sir," he said, "and

demands an immediate interview with you."

General Ferrari turned to Colonel Fuesco.

"You see what trouble you have brought down on my head," he said, with a smile. "I won't bother to see the ambassador now," he said to his orderly. "I shall send these lads to greet him."

In response to these words, Hal and Chester, accompanied by Major Derevaux and Colonel Fuesco, made their way from the room. In the corridor they encountered the American ambassador and Uncle John. The latter was walking back and forth nervously and muttering angrily to himself.

"Here we are, Uncle John," said Chester.

Uncle John jumped as though he had been shot, for he had not perceived their approach.

"You young rascals," he exclaimed, "so you have been released, eh?"

"Yes," said Chester quickly, "we have been released providing we can really apprehend the man who is the spy."

"What do you mean?" asked Uncle John anxiously.

Hal followed Chester's lead, for he wished no obstacle to be put in their path.

"If we can catch the spy, we shall be permitted to go free," he said,

"I see," said Uncle John. "But I can't see that spy-catching is any of your business."

"Well, we have promised to do the best we can," said Chester.

"In that case, I have nothing to say," said Uncle John. "But remember we are due to sail for home to-morrow."

"Oh, we can wait over for the next ship," said Chester.

"Perhaps," said Uncle John, with a twinkle in his eye. "We shall see what your mothers have to say about that."

Hal now bethought himself to introduce Uncle John to his friends. This accomplished, the American ambassador announced that he would be moving, and took his departure. The others Uncle John invited to have lunch with him in a nearby hotel.

Over the table, Hal asked Major Derevaux what he was doing in Rome.

"I don't know as it is my secret now," replied the major. "I am here with a despatch from General Joffre. I cannot say exactly what the despatch contains, but at a guess I would say it has to do with the entrance of Italy into the war, and plans for a possible simultaneous advance between all the troops opposed to the Austro-German army."

"I see," said Hal. "That would be a great thing. I wish we were going back to the front with you."

"Well, you're not," said Uncle John briefly.

"We won't argue about it," said Chester, smiling. "But you never can tell what will happen."

Uncle John changed the subject abruptly. When the conversation reached this stage he always felt uncomfortable.

"When are you going to start spy-hunting?" he asked.

Chester looked at Hal.

"What do you think?" he inquired.

"Well, I should say not until to-night," replied Hal. "I don't believe we could do much good in the day time."

"My idea exactly," agreed Chester. "We may have to make a few preparations."

"I would like to go with you boys," said Major Derevaux, "but I fear it will be impossible. I must return immediately I have had my interview with General Ferrari."

Uncle John had been sitting silent during all this conversation, but now he straightened in his chair and brought his fist down on the table with a bang.

"By Jove!" he exclaimed. "All this talk makes me feel young again. What's the matter with my joining this expedition?"

The two lads gazed at him in wonder. Uncle John saw the amazement written on their features.

"I mean it," he continued. "I want a hand in this game myself. Here, waiter, check!" he called.

He paid the check and rose from the table.

"You wait here for me," he instructed the boys.

"Where are you going?" asked Chester.

"Going to buy a gun," replied Uncle John; "going to outfit

myself to join the spy-hunters."

He stalked from the room.

CHAPTER VI

ON THE TRAIL

The stars were shining when Hal and Chester, accompanied by Uncle John, made their way from the hotel toward the Austrian legation. Uncle John was chuckling to himself as he walked between his two younger companions.

"What is so funny, Uncle John?" asked Chester.

"I was just thinking what your mothers would say if they knew where we were going," was the reply; "particularly if they knew where I was going. I guess they think I am too old for this foolishness, but I tell you, a man likes to be young again."

"What did you tell mother? Where did you say we were going?" asked Hal.

"I told her we were going out—I didn't say where," was the answer. "I'm something of a strategist myself, you know."

"I see you are," replied Chester.

"Now I want you boys to understand that I am under your orders," said Uncle John. "You are older heads at this game than I am. I am willing to obey orders."

"Which is the first essential of every good soldier," said Chester quietly.

"By the way," said Uncle John, patting his pocket, "this is the first time I have had a gun in my hands for a good many years. However, I used to be able to hit the side of a barn. I guess I haven't forgotten. Do you think we shall have to do any shooting?"

"I hope not," said Hal, "but you never can tell."

Uncle John lapsed into silence and the three made their way along slowly. The hour was early, and, as Hal had said, there was no rush.

"Have you formed any definite plan?" asked Chester of Hal, as they walked along.

"Well, no," was the reply. "We shall have to let events shape themselves."

"Which is the best plan, after all," said Chester.

An hour's walk brought them to the embassy building.

"The first thing," said Hal, "is to find out if Robard is in."

"And how are you going to do that?" asked Uncle John.

"Simple," replied Hal. "I'll go up and ask."

He approached the door and rang the bell. A servant opened the door.

"Is Herr Robard in?" asked Hal in perfect German.

The man shook his head.

"I have an important message for him," said Hal. "When shall I find him in?"

The servant glanced at him sharply, then leaned close.

"Are you the messenger Herr Robard expects?" he asked, in a low voice.

Hal glanced sharply about him, more for effect than anything else, and replied, speaking softly:

"From the Wilhelmstrasse."

"Good," said the man, nodding his pleasure. "I am instructed to tell you to come back at a little before ten o'clock."

"Will Herr Robard be here then?"

"Possibly not, but you can wait."

"I shall be here," said Hal, and walked down the steps.

He rejoined Chester and Uncle John, who had waited around the corner.

"I was beginning to fear something had happened to you," said Uncle John.

"What luck?" demanded Chester.

"Better than could be expected," said Hal, and repeated the conversation with the servant.

"And who do you suppose this messenger is?" asked Chester.

"A German secret agent," replied Hal decidedly.

"That was the first thought that flashed through my head when he asked me who I was, which is the reason I took a long chance and mentioned the Wilhelmstrasse."

"You seem to have hit the nail on the head," said Chester.

"Which was luck," said Hal.

"Or quick wit," interposed Uncle John.

"Well," said Chester, "what next? And what are we to do while you are in the house? Surely you are not expecting that we shall all be admitted?"

"No," replied Hal, "and my plan is this: I shall reach the house somewhat earlier than the time set, moving up my watch to avoid suspicion should anything be said. Thus I shall make sure that Robard has not returned. I shall wait.

"Now, when the servant leaves the room, I shall, in some manner, raise the window facing the spot where you stood while I went up to the door a moment ago. Then you and Uncle John can come in. Of course, I may not be left in that particular room to wait, but I shall manage some way. I'll cover your entrance with my gun."

"Good," said Chester, "but then what? Will you try to take the papers forcibly or by stealth?"

"Whichever way seems the most likely to succeed," said Hal briefly. "Something must be left to chance."

"Well," said Chester, "we may as well return to the hotel for a couple of hours. It's early yet."

"Not much," said Uncle John. "I don't want to have to answer any questions. Not me. Let's go some place else."

"We'll walk about, then," Hal decided.

This was done.

At fifteen minutes to ten o'clock Hal once more mounted the steps to the Austrian embassy. Chester and Uncle John took their places at the spot agreed upon, and waited.

The same servant opened the door for Hal.

"You are early," he said, somewhat suspiciously it seemed to Hal.

"Why, no," replied the lad, manifesting surprise. "I am on the dot, as I always am. Ten o'clock."

"But it is not ten yet," said the man.

Hal drew out his watch and looked at it.

"Ten to the minute," he said, and held it up so the man could see.

"Your watch is wrong," was the reply. "However, I suppose it makes no difference. Come in."

He held the door open while Hal entered, then closed it.

"This way," he said, and led the way down the hall. Fortunately, he turned into a room facing upon the street where

Chester and Uncle John waited without, though it was the room beyond the one beneath the window of which they stood. But, Hal noticed, there was a door between the two rooms.

"Ought to be easy enough," he told himself.

"You can wait here for Herr Robard," said the servant, and moved to withdraw.

"This is the Herr Robard's private office, I take it," said Hal.

"You are wrong," was the reply. "His office is just across the hall. But no one is allowed to enter there unless the Herr is with him, and the door is always locked."

"I see," said Hal, mentally thanking the man for the information, which had come a great deal easier than he had expected. "The Herr is a careful man. It is as it should be."

"You can make yourself at home here until he comes," said the servant. "There are magazines and books. I have other matters to attend to."

"All right," said Hal, for he now wished to get rid of the man without more loss of time; he had gained all the information he could hope for without laying himself open to suspicion.

The man withdrew. Hal glanced at his watch.

"Ten-five," he muttered. "That means ten minutes to ten. Robard may come sooner than expected. I must hurry."

Quietly he arose and silently crossed the room. He tried the knob to the door of the next room. The door was locked. He glanced down. There was a key in the lock, and it turned easily. Hal unlocked the door and passed into the room beyond.

Quickly he crossed to the window, and then paused a moment, listening attentively. There was no sound. Unfastening the catch, the lad raised the window gently. It went up without so much as a sound. Hal poked his head out, and called in a low voice:

"All right."

He stepped back and drew his revolver and took his place in the shadow, commanding a view of both doors to the room.

He heard faint sounds without, and concluded rightly that Chester was giving Uncle John a hand up. A moment later Uncle John's head appeared at the window, and he clambered into the room. He was unable to see Hal in the darkness and called:

"Where are you, Hal?"

"Sh—h—h!" whispered Hal. "Come over here."

Uncle John obeyed silently.

There came a whistle from without. Hal recognized it as that of Chester. He hurried to the window and peered out.

"What's the matter?" he called.

"The window is too high, I can't reach the sill," was the reply. "Give me a hand."

Hal started to lay down his gun and lend a hand, but thought better of it. He called to Uncle John.

"Help Chester up," he whispered, and again took his position guarding the doors, with drawn revolver.

Uncle John approached the window and leaned out. He seized Chester's uplifted hand, and pulled. A moment later Chester came scrambling through the window.

"A pretty good climb, if you ask me," he said.

At that moment the door from the hall was thrown open, and a man appeared in the doorway. In his hand he held a revolver, which he pointed straight at Uncle John and Chester, who stood in plain sight before the window.

"Hands up!" he called.

There was nothing for it but to obey. Uncle John's and Chester's hands went high in the air.

Hal, well back from the light which streamed through the open door and the window, slunk further back in the darkness. He was unnoticed, and he knew that he held the whip hand.

"So," said the man in the doorway, "burglars, eh? Well, I shall attend to your cases."

With revolver levelled in a steady hand he advanced further into the room.

CHAPTER VII

UNCLE JOHN IN TROUBLE

A few paces in front of Chester and Uncle John the newcomer paused.

"Armed?" he asked.

Chester made no reply. Uncle John remained silent.

"We'll see," said the newcomer briefly.

Still covering them with his weapon, he put his free hand in Chester's pocket and relieved the lad of his revolver. A similar operation and Uncle John's gun came forth. Uncle John could keep quiet no longer.

"There goes my gun," he said sorrowfully.

In spite of the seriousness of the situation Chester was forced to laugh.

"Don't worry; you'll get it back," he replied.

"You think so, eh?" sneered the newcomer. "Tell me," addressing Chester, "what are you doing here?"

"That's for you to find out," replied the lad.

"Well, I'll find out," exclaimed the man. "Do you know who I am?"

"Why, yes; your name is Robard, isn't it?"

The other stepped back in surprise.

"So you know me, eh!" he exclaimed. "Then you are not burglars."

"Hardly," replied Chester.

"Then what are you doing here?"

"I can't see that it will do any harm to tell you," was Chester's answer. "We are after the paper you stole from Colonel Fuesco to-day."

"Oho! And by any chance are you the same youngster I encountered in the street?"

"The same," replied Chester briefly.

"And where is the other? Surely," peering closely at Uncle John, "you are not he. He was younger."

"Right you are," replied Uncle John. "But I guess he'll turn up when he is most needed."

"You think so? Then he had better turn up quickly." He turned again to Chester. "So you came after the paper," he said. "I am very sorry to say that you will not get it."

"Then you have sent it to Vienna," said Chester, somewhat crestfallen.

"Oh, no, I still have it right here," and Robard tapped the breast pocket of his coat.

"Thanks," said Chester. "I just wanted to know where you kept it."

"I suppose you think you are very smart," said the Austrian, somewhat angry at having betrayed himself.

"Smart enough, I guess," returned Chester.

"Come, I have had enough of this," exclaimed the Austrian. "Hold your hands up now, and march out of this room ahead of me."

He waved his revolver from one to the other, and stepped aside that the two might pass ahead of him. Uncle John and Chester obeyed his injunction and moved toward the door. The Austrian took a step after them.

It was at this moment that Hal came into action.

With a sudden spring he leaped upon the Austrian from behind. With one hand he seized the wrist that held the revolver, and turned it upward. With the other he clutched the man by the throat, shutting off his wind and preventing him from crying out. Hal called to Chester:

"Grab him!"

Chester and Uncle John wheeled about and lent a hand in subduing the Austrian. Three against one, it was easy work, and after a short struggle Robard lay panting on the floor.

Hal drew his own revolver and covered him.

"One move and you are a dead man," he said quietly.

Robard glared up at him angrily. Chester smiled at him pleasantly.

"You see I am smarter than you gave me credit for," he said.

The Austrian made no response.

"He keeps the paper in his pocket, Hal," said Chester.

"So I heard him say," replied Hal.

He bent over the Austrian and thrust a hand into his pocket. He pulled forth a batch of papers, and walking over to the window, ran through them hurriedly.

"Find it?" asked Chester, walking over to him.

Hal extended a paper.

"I guess this is it, all right," he said, and thrust the document into his pocket.

At that moment there came a startled cry from Uncle John, followed by a heavy thud. Hal and Chester wheeled quickly, just in time to see Robard disappearing through the door, which closed after him with a bang. A key turned in the lock. The thud they had heard was Uncle John toppling to the floor as the result of a blow delivered by the Austrian, who, catching Uncle John off his guard, had sprung to his feet and attacked him.

Hal jumped to the door, while Chester bent over Uncle John

and assisted him to his feet.

"The scoundrel!" exclaimed Uncle John. "He took me by surprise. He gave me no warning."

"Surely you didn't expect him to," said Chester, somewhat angry.

Hal sprang to Chester's side.

"Quick!" he exclaimed. "We must get out of here. Robard will have assistance in a moment."

"Which way? Out the window?" asked Chester.

"I guess that will be the best way," said Hal. "You first, Uncle John."

The three hurried to the window, and Uncle John put a leg over the sill. As he did so a sharp shot rang out and Uncle John withdrew his leg hurriedly. He tumbled over to the floor, and seizing his foot in his hand, rocked himself back and forward.

"Hit?" asked Chester anxiously.

"I'm afraid so," replied Uncle John, apparently very much frightened.

Chester bent over him.

He looked at the heel of Uncle John's shoe, and then exclaimed.

"Get up. You are all right. The bullet just carried your heel away."

Uncle John rose to his feet.

"Felt like I had been plugged through the leg," he said. "Just the shock, I guess. Well, what now, boys? We can't get out that way."

"We'll have to go through the door, then," said Chester.

He approached and tried the knob.

"It's locked," said Hal. "I tried it a moment ago. However, that's the way we shall have to go out. Stand back a little."

He drew his revolver, put the muzzle to the lock and fired. There was a loud explosion and the room filled with smoke. Hal seized the knob and threw the door open.

"Where are your guns?" he asked Chester hurriedly.

"Robard took them," replied Chester.

"Then they must be in the room. Find them quickly."

Chester looked hurriedly about. At last his eyes lighted upon them, on a little table at the far end of the room, where the Austrian had laid them.

"All right," said Chester, picking them up and passing one to Uncle John. "The sooner we make a start the better."

"Let's go then," said Hal.

He poked his head cautiously out the door and looked down the hall. There was no one in sight.

"Coast clear," he called over his shoulder. "Follow me!"

He sprang into the hall and started for the front door on a dead run. Chester was right behind him, and Uncle John followed close upon Chester's heels.

Hal was just about to seize the knob in his free hand, when it was turned from the outside.

"Back, quick," called the lad. "Some one coming."

He wheeled about as he spoke and the other two did like-wise. They had barely regained their retreat when heavy footsteps were heard in the hall.

"This way," called a voice in German.

The footsteps came toward them, stopped before the door a moment, and then passed on.

"Now for another trial," whispered Hal.

Again he poked his head out and saw that the coast was apparently clear.

"Come on!" he cried, and made a second dash for the front door. Chester followed him, as did Uncle John.

This time Hal reached the door without trouble and threw it open. Without pausing, he dashed through it and down the steps. Chester was right behind him. But as Uncle John also would have passed out, there came a shot from behind and he toppled to the floor.

In the excitement neither Chester nor Hal noticed this and they had gone half a block before they discovered that Uncle John was not with them.

"Great Scott! What can have happened to him?" exclaimed Chester.

"Probably got caught," replied Hal.

"Then we must go back after him. Come on."

"Wait a minute," said Hal. "Don't forget this paper we recovered. It must be returned to General Ferrari, Uncle John or no Uncle John."

"But we can't let them kill him!" cried Chester.

"They won't kill him," said Hal positively. "They would be afraid to do that. First I must deliver this paper, and then we shall try to rescue Uncle John. But the paper is first. You know that."

"You are right, of course," Chester agreed. "Besides Uncle John knew what he was up against before he came with us. He'll have to wait until we can help him."

"All right, then. Now my idea is for you to wait here while I return this paper to General Ferrari. Then I shall come back and we will see what can be done. If they should take Uncle John from the house you follow them."

"Suits me," said Chester. "Get back as soon as you can."

Hal waved a hand and hurried away in the darkness.

"Guess I'll see if I can learn anything," said Chester to himself, after Hal had disappeared.

He approached the embassy cautiously. He could see lights within, but the shades were drawn and he could distinguish nothing. Once he thought he heard sounds of a struggle in the house, but he could not be sure.

He was on the point of entering, but it occurred to him that if he should fall into the enemy's hands he could do Uncle John little good.

"I'll wait until Hal comes back, anyhow," he decided at last.

He walked some distance from the embassy, still remaining close enough to see any one who should leave by the front door, and sat down on the steps before a large stone house.

"Hope Hal gets a move on," he muttered to himself, as he settled himself as comfortably as possible.

Clair W. Hayes

CHAPTER VIII

UNCLE JOHN SHOWS HIS METTLE

When Uncle John fell to the floor, his first feeling was one of anger. He scarcely felt the sharp pain in his leg, where a bullet had grazed the skin. He saw Chester disappearing ahead of him, and his first thought was to get up and hurry after him.

He pulled himself to his feet and again moved toward the door. As he did so he felt a pair of arms thrown about him from behind. Uncle John turned to give battle to this assailant.

Now Uncle John was a big man and in his youth had been noted for his strength. Time had sapped his prowess, however, and he knew that he was no match for his adversary. Nevertheless, he determined to fight it out.

With an effort he shook off the encircling arms and faced his opponent, who proved to be none other than Robard himself. Bethinking himself of the days of his youth, when he had been considered something of a boxer, Uncle John decided to keep the other at arm's length, if possible. Therefore he squared off in most approved fashion.

It was plain that the Austrian was not an exponent of the art of self-defense and Uncle John sent three hard blows to the man's face, before the latter stepped back and sought to bring his revolver to bear. But Uncle John had no mind to be shot down and he sprang forward and seized the other in a fierce embrace. This style of fighting was more to the Austrian's liking.

A big man himself, he was nothing loath to test Uncle John's wrestling ability. He threw his arms about him, and the two struggled up and down the long hall, panting and gasping.

But the Austrian was a younger man and he soon realized that Uncle John was beginning to tire. The latter realized it also and knew that if he would be successful, it must be immediately. He put a foot in back of the Austrian and pushed hard. Robard lost his balance and fell, but he kept his grip, and Uncle John was pulled to the floor with him.

Uncle John freed an arm and planted his fist squarely in the Austrian's face. The latter gave a cry of rage and shouted for help. Uncle John smiled grimly.

"You'll need it," he said.

Again he raised a fist and brought it down with all his force. The Austrian's arms relaxed their grip. He quivered a bit, and then sank back unconscious. Uncle John got to his feet.

"I'm not so bad at that," he told himself modestly. "I wish the boys could have been here to see that. Now to get out of here."

He moved toward the door, but even as he would have opened it, it moved back and three men stepped inside. They saw Uncle John and the unconscious form of Robard at first

Clair W. Hayes

glance, and sprang upon Uncle John with a shout.

Uncle John drew a long breath and waded into the midst of them.

The newcomers also proved to be novices in the fistic art, and as long as Uncle John was able to keep them at long range he gave a good account of himself. But, realizing that they were getting the worst of this kind of fighting, one of the men gave a command to close in. In vain Uncle John strove to keep them off. One threw himself to the floor, and avoiding a heavy kick, grasped Uncle John by the leg, pulling him down. The others piled on top of him.

Two minutes later Uncle John had ceased to struggle, and lay powerless in the hands of his captors.

"Well, you've got me," he said. "Now what?"

Still keeping a tight grip upon him, the men assisted Uncle John to his feet. One drew a revolver and covered him. The other two went to the assistance of Robard, who was just getting to his feet. The latter came forward with an angry gleam in his eye.

"So I've got you at last," he said. "Well, I'll see that you don't get away this time."

"You weren't big enough to get me alone," said Uncle John, panting from his exertions.

"I wasn't, eh!" shouted Robard, now furiously angry. "I've got you now, and you shall pay. Take that!"

He dealt Uncle John a heavy blow with the back of his hand.

In his early days Uncle John had been noted for his fiery temper. It was said of him that when his temper was aroused, he became a maniac. So it was now.

Taking no thought of the man who held the revolver almost in his face, Uncle John, his cheek red from the imprint of the Austrian's hand, uttered a cry of rage, and leaped forward. His move was so unexpected that the man with the revolver did not fire, and when at last he had again brought his revolver to bear, he feared to press the trigger lest he might hit his friend as well as foe.

Uncle John, in a moment, was the center of a struggling, shouting mass. His fists flew about like flails and he kicked out with his feet whenever occasion presented itself. One, two, three heavy blows he landed upon Robard's face, and the Austrian suddenly collapsed in a heap. Still fighting mad, Uncle John whirled upon the other three, who now closed with him.

A right-handed jolt caught one of them flush on the jaw and he toppled over backwards without so much as a groan. The other brought a fist heavily to Uncle John's nose, bringing blood, but before he could repeat the blow, Uncle John had placed him hors de combat with a terrific left-handed punch to the abdomen.

Then the third man drew back and presented his revolver, but Uncle John sprang forward with a cry and before the man's finger could press the trigger, Uncle John had seized him about the middle. Raising him high in the air, he swung him to one side, and the man's head struck the wall with a crunch even as the revolver exploded.

Uncle John dropped the limp body and surveyed the field. His anger had departed and he was again a cool and

Clair W. Hayes

self-possessed American gentleman of middle age.

"There's that temper of mine again," he said reprovingly to himself. "Why, I might have killed somebody. After all these years I should have it under control. I guess I'll be moving before some one makes me real mad."

He stooped and picked up his hat, which had fallen on the floor, took one last look at his fallen foes, and opened the door and passed out.

Down the street he saw a solitary figure sitting upon the steps in front of a large stone house, and he walked in the other direction.

"I've had trouble enough for one night," he told himself. "Guess I will give that fellow a wide berth."

And had he gone toward the seated figure he would have avoided more trouble for all concerned, and Hal and Chester would probably never have seen active service with the Italian army. For the figure that caused Uncle John to turn his footsteps in the opposite direction was Chester, awaiting the return of Hal.

"Wonder why those young scalawags didn't come back to help me?" mused Uncle John, as he walked along toward the hotel. "I'll tell them what I think of them for running away and leaving me to do all the fighting."

Uncle John glanced at his watch.

"Great Scott!" he exclaimed. "Twelve o'clock! Why, it doesn't seem fifteen minutes since we went in that house. Guess Hal and Chester have returned to the hotel by this time. What shall I tell the women folks? They'll wonder what a man of my age is prowling about the streets of Rome for at this hour of the night."

He entered his hotel and made his way toward the elevator. It descended, and as he would have entered, he bumped squarely into Mrs. Paine and Mrs. Crawford.

"John," cried the latter, "where is Chester?"

"Where is Hal?" demanded Mrs. Paine anxiously.

"Why, they—aren't they—they'll be here in a few minutes," stuttered Uncle John.

"Where are they?" demanded the two anxious mothers in a single voice.

"Now hold on here," said Uncle John, regaining his composure with an effort. "I'll explain. Hal and Chester are all right. They'll be here in a few minutes."

"And what on earth is the matter with you, John?" asked Mrs. Crawford in surprise.

"What's the matter with me?"

"Yes. Your collar is half off, your clothes are dirty and there is blood on your shoe. What is the matter?"

"Well, nothing much," replied Uncle John in great confusion, "you see, I had—I had a—"

"And were Hal and Chester with you?" asked Mrs. Paine.

"Yes, that is no. I mean—" stuttered Uncle John.

"Come now, John, no fibbing," said Mrs. Crawford. "You were in trouble, and Hal and Chester were with you. Where are they now?"

"Well, to tell the truth, I don't know where they are," said Uncle John. "I supposed they would be here by this time."

In a few words he explained what had transpired.

"They left the house without being hurt?" asked Mrs. Paine.

"Yes, ma'am."

"Then where can they be now?" demanded Mrs. Crawford.

"I'm sure I don't know, unless they have stopped for a talk with the general, and that's about the size of it."

"I guess you are right," replied Mrs. Paine with relief. "But why didn't you tell us all this before you went out to-night?"

"Yes, why didn't you?" demanded Mrs. Crawford.

"Well," said Uncle John slowly, "we didn't want to worry you."

"You are getting too old for such foolishness," declared Mrs. Crawford.

"I thought so myself," replied Uncle John, "but I know better now. If you had seen the licking I handed those four Austrians you would think I was a boy again."

"I'll think you have reached your second childhood if you ever let me hear of anything like it again," declared his sister.

Uncle John was growing tired of this conversation. He wanted to be let alone.

"I'll go out and see if I can find the boys," he said.

"Please do," said Mrs. Paine.

"And see that you keep out of mischief yourself," adjured Mrs. Crawford.

Uncle John shook his head as he walked away.

"These women are funny things," he said. "I wonder what can have happened to those boys? They've probably gone back to look for me. Guess I had better head that way myself. I may come in handy, you never can tell."

He patted the revolver, which still rested securely in his pocket.

"I may have use for this next time," he muttered, as he quickened his steps toward the Austrian legation.

CHAPTER IX

CAPTURED

Chester rose to his feet, as he saw a figure hurrying toward him.

"Must be Hal," he said.

He was right. A moment later Hal came up to him.

"Did you give the general the paper?" asked Chester.

"Yes. Any one come out of the house?"

"I haven't seen any one, and I have been right here all the time you were gone."

"Hear any sounds from within?"

"Thought I did several times, but I couldn't be sure. Thought I heard a shot once."

"Well, we had better go and have a look. I don't believe they will harm Uncle John, but he probably is beginning to be worried by this time."

He led the way and Chester followed him. Hal mounted the steps without hesitancy and turned the knob of the door. The door opened and the lad stepped inside, where he halted with a cry of surprise. Chester peered over his shoulder.

"Looks like a cyclone had struck this place," Hal ejaculated.

It did indeed. Robard was lying upon the floor, with a man on either side of him, and a fourth lay some distance away, his skull crushed in.

"Uncle John probably was the cyclone," said Chester briefly. "I have heard that he used to be considerable of a fighter in his younger days."

"And still he could hardly have done all this," said Hal.

"Remember Alexis," said Chester sententiously.

"That's different," replied Hal.

"Well, maybe so, but—"

Chester broke off and grabbed Hal by the arm.

"Sh-h-h," he whispered.

Hal listened attentively for a few seconds. The faint sound of footsteps could be heard approaching from further back in the house. At the same moment Robard groaned, moved about and sat up. The hands of the two lads dropped to their pockets.

But before they could draw their weapons, they were startled by a voice behind them.

Clair W. Hayes

"Hands up!" it said.

There was no mistaking the menace in the quiet tones and Hal and Chester realized that the owner of the voice meant business.

"Good work, Fritz," came the voice of Robard, and he pulled himself to his feet with some difficulty and advanced toward the boys. "I'll thank you for your guns," he said. "No, I'll get them myself," he added as both boys moved their hands toward the weapons.

He suited the action to the word and relieved the lads of their automatics.

"Now stand back there against the wall," he commanded.

The boys obeyed.

Robard now gave his attention to the injured men on the floor. Two of them showed signs of returning consciousness and soon were able to get to their feet. The other could not be revived, and at a command from Robard, he was carried to another room.

"Well, I've got you this time," said Robard to Hal and Chester, "and this time I'll guarantee you don't get away."

"I wouldn't be too sure of that," said Hal with a smile. "We are pretty hard to hold on to."

"I'll hold on to you, never fear," was the response. "I'd like to get my hands on the other."

"Then he has gotten away?" queried Chester.

"Oh, yes, he got away all right," said Robard with a frown. "He's as strong as an ox, and a real fighter."

"Then he was responsible for all this human wreckage we found when we came in?" demanded Hal.

"He was," was the grim reply, "but the next time I get my hands on him there will be a different story to tell. Why, he's a madman when he gets started."

"Then I would advise you to keep away from him," said Hal.

The sound of footsteps outside the door prevented Robard from replying. Levelling a revolver at the lads, he motioned them to be silent, and took up a position at the side of the hall, where he would be concealed by the door when it swung inward.

A hand turned the knob and the door swung back. Uncle John's face appeared in the doorway. He saw Hal and Chester immediately and advanced with a smile.

"So here you are," he said. "Your mothers—"

The sentence died on his lips as Robard, who had stepped quietly from behind the door, brought the butt of his heavy revolver down upon his head. Uncle John dropped to the floor like a log.

The action had been so sudden that neither Hal nor Chester had time to give a cry of warning, though both would have done so, in spite of Robard's command for them to remain quiet. As Uncle John fell, Chester stepped forward, but he was confronted by the barrel of Robard's gun.

"Stand back," said the Austrian.

Chester obeyed. There was nothing else he could do in the face of certain death should he refuse.

Now Robard called two of his men, and Uncle John was carried into an adjoining room. Robard motioned Hal and Chester in also.

Uncle John was laid upon the bed, and at a command from Robard, was tightly bound. Hal and Chester were also tied to chairs, after which Robard took his leave, saying:

"I'll see you the first thing in the morning."

"What are you going to do with us?" demanded Chester.

"I haven't decided yet," was the reply. "But wait. If you will return me the paper you took from me I shall let you all go now."

"It's too late," said Hal quietly. "I gave the paper to General Ferrari."

"I had surmised as much," said Robard. "Well, good-night."

He waved a hand airily and stepped from the room. Then he turned and poked his head back through the door.

"A word more," he said. "In case you should unloose your bonds, I would advise you not to try to escape. There will be a man on guard here in the hall all night, and another outside, so you cannot leave by the window."

"Thanks," said Hal dryly.

Robard withdrew his head and a key grated in the lock.

"Well, now what are we going to do?" asked Hal.

"You've got me," replied Chester. "Say, do you know this reminds me of old times—of the days in France, Belgium and Russia."

"You bet," agreed Hal, "and those were the good old days."

At this juncture Uncle John moaned feebly and his eyelids fluttered. A moment later the lids opened and he gazed at Hal and Chester curiously. Then the light of comprehension dawned upon his face and he spoke:

"So they have got us all, eh?"

"Yes, they've got us," replied Chester.

"The trouble will be to keep us," said Hal. "How do you feel, sir?"

"Not much," replied Uncle John. "What did he hit me with, a crowbar?"

"No, just a revolver butt," replied Chester, grinning.

"How did they happen to capture you boys?"

"We came back here looking for you, as soon as Hal had delivered the paper to General Ferrari," Chester explained.

"Your mothers are worried almost to death," said Uncle John.

"I'm afraid they will worry a whole lot more before we get out of here," said Chester. "I don't know what Robard will do with us."

"Perhaps we may see the Austrian ambassador," said Hal hopefully. "Certainly he would stand for no such work as this."

"I don't know about that," said Chester. "They are likely to all be alike."

"Well, we shall just have to make the best of it," said Hal.

"By the way, Uncle John," said Chester, "you must be considerable of a fighter. You laid these fellows out in great shape a while ago."

"I did do a pretty fair job," admitted his uncle, "but they made me mad."

"I vote that we try to get a little sleep," said Hal. "It won't be very comfortable here in these chairs, but we shall have to make the best of it. Perhaps with the coming of daylight something will turn up."

Chester tugged at his bonds in vain.

"Can't budge 'em," he said.

Hal closed his eyes.

"I'm going to try to get forty winks," he said. "Good night."

Chester followed his friend's example, and Uncle John also composed himself to sleep. And in spite of their uncomfortable positions, presently all slumbered.

Hal was the first to awaken. The key turning in the lock of the door aroused him. Sunlight streamed in through the closed window. The face of Robard appeared in the door, and he entered the room.

"Good morning," he said.

At the sound of his voice, Chester and Uncle John opened their eyes.

"Good morning," replied Hal. "I trust you have come to liberate us."

"Of your bonds, yes," was the reply; "but I regret to say that I cannot set you free."

"What are you going to do with us?"

"Take you to Austria."

"To Austria! Great Scott! What for?"

"For no particular reason," said Robard, and his face suddenly took on a savage look, "except that you have thwarted me, and for that you shall pay. I shall probably lose my rank for my failure to obtain the papers, and if I do I want some one to take my spite out on. Do I make myself clear?"

"Perfectly," replied Hal quietly. "It is very like a coward."

Robard took a threatening step forward.

"A coward, am I?" he cried in a loud voice.

He made as though to strike the lad, then suddenly changed his mind.

"I'll wait," he said. "I promise you shall regret those words before I am through with you."

"And when do we start?" asked Chester.

"To-night; after dark. A special train will be ready for the Austrian ambassador and his suite. You shall go with us. Of course the ambassador shall know nothing of your presence, for he would not permit me to work out a personal grudge in this way. I shall keep you out of his sight."

"The ambassador has been given his passports then?" asked Chester.

"He has, to Italy's sorrow. We shall wipe her off the map."

"Don't forget you have a pretty sizable job on your hands already," said Hal.

Robard made no reply, but turning on his heel, strode from the room.

CHAPTER X

VENICE

As the boys had feared, they were given no opportunity to make a personal appeal to the Austrian ambassador. All day long they were kept in their improvised prison. They slept a little and talked a little, but try as they would they were unable to so much as loosen their bonds. But they all agreed on one thing, as expressed by Chester:

"We'll make a break for freedom at the first opportunity, no matter what the odds against us."

One of Robard's hirelings brought them a bite to eat about noon and again shortly after 6 o'clock. Darkness fell and still Robard himself had failed to appear.

"Maybe the time for departure has been postponed," said Chester.

"Hardly," replied Uncle John. "If the ambassador has been given his passports and has made arrangements to leave Italy he'll probably go at the appointed time."

It was at this juncture that footsteps were heard without. The key turned in the lock and a moment later Robard stood

Clair W. Hayes

before them.

"Well," he said cheerfully, "all ready for your little trip?"

"We're not what you would call ready," replied Hal, with an attempt at levity, "but if you say it's time to move, we may as well agree with you."

"Your reasoning is to be commended," said Robard. He step-ped to the door and raised his voice in a shout. A moment later a second man stood beside him. "Untie these fellows while I keep them covered," he ordered, at the same time producing a brace of automatics.

The man stepped forward and with a few quick movements relieved the prisoners of their bonds. He stepped back.

"Stand up!" commanded Robard, levelling his revolvers, "and mind, no tricks."

Hal, Chester and Uncle John obeyed. It was a wonderful relief to be on their feet again and be able to stretch their cramped muscles.

"By George! this feels better," said Chester.

"Rather," agreed Hal dryly.

Robard moved to one side of the room.

"Out you go," he said, motioning toward the door with his revolver, but still keeping the three covered.

"Which way?" asked Hal, playing for time.

"Out the door is all you need to know," was the reply.

"You'll find pleasant company there."

One of the revolvers covered Hal threateningly.

Hal walked toward the door, followed by Chester and then Uncle John. Robard followed close behind, with his man at his heels.

Outside the door Hal led the way down the hall toward the front door, where he saw perhaps half a dozen other figures standing about. These proved to be more Austrians. Near the door Hal halted at a word of command from Robard and the three prisoners soon were surrounded. Their captors were all dressed in civilian attire, but from their military bearings, Hal and Chester concluded that they were Austrian army officers.

Robard turned to one who stood somewhat apart from the others.

"Everything ready?" he asked.

"All ready," was the reply. "The baggage has been sent on ahead of us and the train to Venice will leave within the hour."

"Good! And the ambassador?"

"Will be here within half an hour," was the answer.

Hal's heart leaped. Here, he thought, would be a chance to demand his freedom, and that of his companions. He was loath to believe that a man in the capacity of an ambassador would countenance such proceedings. But his hopes were doomed to disappointment.

Within the half hour mentioned, the door was flung suddenly open and a small man hurried in. He gazed quickly about him and then spoke to Robard.

"Everything ready?" he asked.

"Yes, sir," was Robard's answer.

The ambassador—for such the newcomer was—gazed rapidly about him. His eyes rested on Hal, Chester and Uncle John.

"Who are these?" he demanded with a wave of his hand in their direction.

"These," said Robard, taking a step forward, and throwing a warning look at the three prisoners, "are a trio who have too much knowledge of some of our plans. I thought it best to take them along, sir."

Hal took a quick step forward, but even as he opened his mouth to speak, he felt something cold pressed against the back of his neck by a hand from behind. He closed his lips and fell back.

The ambassador was silent a moment before replying. Then he said:

"You are sure you are not taking too much upon yourself? You are certain you are right in your surmise?"

"It is not a surmise, sir; it is a fact," returned Robard.

For another moment the ambassador hesitated. Then he said with a shrug of his shoulders:

"Very well then. Come; let us go."

He led the way out the door, the others following. Hal, Chester and Uncle John were kept closely in the center of the little knot of men as all made their way down the steps to where three large automobiles stood waiting at the curb. The ambassador and Robard climbed into the first, and Hal found himself separated from his friends as he was pushed into the second machine; Chester and Uncle John were in the third.

Twenty minutes later the three prisoners found themselves in a first class section on the special express for Venice, vigilantly guarded by two Austrians, who had been placed in charge of them after they had been securely tied up at Robard's command. Robard himself had entered another compartment with the ambassador.

"You'll be safer this way," the Austrian had said with a smile, after testing their bonds to make sure they were secure.

"Looks like we were pretty safe any way you might put us," replied Hal grimly.

"You Americans are pretty slippery customers; I won't take any chances with you," was the rejoinder, and Robard took his leave.

A few moments later a slight motion told the prisoners that the train had started.

"Well, here we go," said Chester with a laugh. "We've been started for the enemy's country in this manner before."

"Only on previous occasions our destination was Berlin instead of Venice," replied Hal.

"Which is not our destination after all," said Uncle John. "Our true destination is back to the hotel where we left your mothers."

"And I am sure we shall reach it eventually," said Hal hopefully.

"How long does it take to get to Venice?" asked Chester.

"I don't know exactly," replied Uncle John. "But we shall be there by daylight surely."

"Perhaps we may get a chance to make a break for liberty," said Chester.

"Don't bank on that, Chester," replied Hal. "It looks as though these fellows do things a little more thoroughly than their German cousins. Still there is always a chance."

"While there's life there's hope, eh?" said Uncle John. "We'll see."

"In the meantime," said Hal, "we may as well try to get a little sleep."

"A good idea," agreed Chester. "Here goes."

He closed his eyes and was soon in the land of dreams. Hal and Uncle John followed suit.

How long they slept they did not know, but they were awakened by rough hands shaking them and the sound of gruff voices. Hal opened his eyes. Daylight streamed in through the windows of the compartment.

"Get up!" commanded a harsh voice.

Hal rubbed his eyes and called to Chester and Uncle John.

"What's the matter?" asked the latter sleepily.

"Venice, I guess," was the reply.

Again their bonds were removed, and under cover of the revolvers of their captors, which the latter kept concealed in their coats but which the three prisoners knew were ever ready, Hal, Chester and Uncle John stepped from the car.

The Austrian ambassador and Robard had alighted before them, and Hal could see them talking and gesticulating excitedly.

"Wonder what's up?" he muttered.

"Which way from here, do you suppose?" asked Chester.

"Trieste, I should say," replied Uncle John. "They will want to get over the border as soon as possible, and I guess they will head in that direction."

"My idea, too," agreed Hal.

What was their surprise, then, when, instead of boarding another train, as Hal had confidently believed would be done, the ambassador led the way into the station and then to the street beyond. Here Robard disappeared for a brief moment, and returning, motioned the ambassador and others to follow him.

Again the prisoners found themselves shoved into a large touring car, which started immediately in the wake of the one which bore Robard and the ambassador.

Clair W. Hayes

"Some funny business here, as sure as you're born," said Chester excitedly.

"Must be," declared Hal grimly. "Robard and the ambassador have something up their sleeves. Wonder if the Italian authorities are not on their guard. There is no telling what these fellows may do."

"I don't imagine the Italian authorities are watching them any too closely," remarked Uncle John. "You know men in such positions are supposed to be men of honor."

"Which the ambassador undoubtedly is," said Chester. "If there is anything wrong, you can take my word that Robard is the gentleman who is responsible for it."

"You have hit the nail on the head there, old fellow," agreed Hal.

After a ten-minute drive the machine came to an abrupt stop.

"Out you go," said a gruff voice in very poor English.

It was the voice of one of their captors and the prisoners obeyed.

Ahead, the ambassador and Robard were walking down the steps to the canal, and a few moments later a large closed gondola came toward them.

The ambassador entered, followed by Robard, and the prisoners found themselves aboard also a moment later. The gondola moved off.

"Well, what next?" demanded Chester.

"It's too deep for me," was the reply. "But we are going to learn something; that's sure. Perhaps it's a good thing we were captured and brought along. Who knows? we may be able to avert some mischief."

"Let us sincerely hope so," said Uncle John earnestly. "I know that you boys are experienced in this line of work, but you can count on me to the last ditch."

"You didn't need to tell us that, Uncle John," said Chester. "We knew it."

The gondola stopped.

Clair W. Hayes

CHAPTER XI

A PLOT IS FOILED

"Out with you," commanded one of their captors, when he saw that the ambassador and Robard had made their way up the short flight of steps.

No urging was necessary. The prisoners, closely followed by their guards, made their way in the same direction. A hundred yards ahead, they were suddenly turned to the left, where they caught sight of a small house. Into this they were marched and then on into a room at the far end of the short hall.

"Guess you'll be safe enough in there. No need to tie you up," said the voice of Robard, who came up at this moment.

The door slammed, a key grated harshly and the prisoners were left alone.

"Now what in the name of all that's wonderful do you suppose this means?" asked Chester. "Think they are going to leave us here to starve or perish of thirst?"

"No, I guess not," was the reply. "My opinion is that Robard is up to something funny, and that he has enticed the ambassador here on some pretext or another."

"What do you think he is up to?" demanded Chester.

"If I knew I'd have told you a long while ago," said Hal. "Now, if we—"

He paused as Chester held up a warning hand. The latter moved toward the wall at the far end of the room as Hal eyed him curiously. The lad placed his ear against the wall, and listened intently for a moment; then he motioned Hal and Uncle John to approach.

"The ambassador and Robard are in the next room," he whispered. "I can hear them talking. Listen."

Hal and Uncle John also laid their ears to the wall.

"But," and the ambassador's voice came faintly to them, "such a thing as you suggest is dishonorable."

"What has that to do with it, sir?" came Robard's reply. "Our enemies would do the same thing had they the opportunity. All's fair in war, you know, sir."

"Not that," said the ambassador. "You must remember that until I have crossed the frontier I am still the ambassador to Italy. I am upon my honor to leave the country peaceably."

"But no one would know you had a hand in the matter, sir."

"That is not the point," was the reply.

"But I have made all arrangements," protested Robard. "Everything is ready. The chief of the Italian general staff is in Venice at this moment, and at noon will inspect the large stores of ammunition at the northern outskirts of the city. A word from you and ammunition, chief of staff and all will be destroyed."

"I will give no such word," was the angry response. "Besides," and the ambassador considered a moment, "why do you wish a word from me in this matter? It could have been done without my consent."

"Well, sir, I—we—I," stammered Robard, evidently at a loss for a convincing reply.

There came the sound of a blow, as though a hand had struck a table and the ambassador's voice rose angrily.

"Robard," he said sternly, "I can see through your plot. You would have me stand sponsor for this crime, that you might disqualify me upon my return to Vienna."

"I assure you, sir—" began Robard.

"Enough," replied the ambassador. "I have not forgotten that you were ever my enemy—at least until this war brought us closer together and put an end to all our disputes—at least, so I believed. Now I know better."

"Sir—" Robard began again.

"I have told you I would have no hand in it," declared the ambassador. "What is more, I forbid it! Do you understand, I forbid it!"

Now Robard's voice rose angrily.

"You forbid it!" he exclaimed. "You forbid it! Well, little good will that do. I will see that the work is carried out if I have to do it myself. And what is more, I will see that the blame falls on you. You are right. I have plotted to discredit you, and I shall do it, or my name is not Robard."

"I shall see that your actions are brought to the attention of the emperor," declared the ambassador. "And more than that, I shall immediately notify the Italian authorities of your plans, that they may be on their guard."

"You will never do that," replied Robard, and his voice was so low that the listeners could scarcely catch the words.

"Robard," said the ambassador sternly, "you may consider yourself under arrest."

There was the sound of a scraping chair and heavy footsteps moving in the room beyond.

"Another move and I shall fire," came Robard's voice.

"Man, you don't know what you are doing," came the surprised voice of the ambassador.

"Don't?" said Robard, with a sneer in his voice. "I'll show you."

Again there came to the listeners' ears the sounds of heavy footsteps, followed by the noise of a struggle.

"Great Scott! They are fighting!" exclaimed Hal. "What can we do? He might kill the Ambassador."

"There is nothing we can do, old man," replied Chester quietly. "We'll have to let them fight it out."

They listened intently.

The struggle continued, and occasionally the listeners could catch the sound of fierce ejaculations. Then, suddenly, there came the sound of a shot. Then silence, followed a moment later by a voice:

"There! I guess now you will know better than to interfere with me."

"Robard," said the voice of the ambassador, very weak now, "you shall pay for this."

"I don't know whether I have done for you or not," came Robard's voice after a pause, "and I don't care. In fact, I hope I have. Now, just to blacken your reputation a bit, if I have killed you, I shall go through with my plan."

The boys could hear him stalk heavily across the room. A moment later a door slammed.

Hal rose to his feet and passed a hand across a moist brow.

"And to think that we were unable to lend a hand," he muttered.

"He's a black villain," declared Uncle John.

"And now," said Chester, "he is on his errand of mischief. Can we do nothing to thwart him?"

"I can't see how," declared Uncle John.

"Nor I," said Hal.

"Wait a moment, though," said Chester.

"Well?" queried Hal anxiously.

"I think it can be done," replied Chester quietly. "At least there is a chance."

"Let's have it," demanded Hal eagerly.

"Well, here is the idea. We'll stir up a racket in here. Naturally some of our captors will come to see what it is all about. We won't quiet down until he opens the door. Now you will notice that the door swings inward. That will help. Also that from outside it is impossible to see this side of the room. I'll stand behind the door. You and Uncle John remain on this side and stay here until the man comes into the room. Then I'll jump him, or them, as the case may be."

"But they'll get you, Chester," said Uncle John.

"Perhaps," was the reply. "That's the chance I must take. But we can't let a little thing like that stand in the way. As soon as I tackle them, or him, you two can rush out and lend a hand. There'll be a hard fight, of course, and the first fellow that gets a chance to make a break through the door will do so. Do I make myself clear?"

"Perfectly," said Hal. "And the plan is not so bad. There is a certain chance of success."

"Well, it doesn't look good to me," replied Uncle John. "One of you boys is almost sure to get killed."

"You are taking the same chance, sir," replied Chester.

"Oh, I'm not worrying about myself," returned Uncle John. "But you must remember that I am to some extent responsible for you and I shall have to answer to your mothers for your safety."

"If you wish," said Chester dryly, "we'll each write you a little note exonerating you of all blame should either of us be hurt."

Uncle John was forced to smile.

"Oh, never mind," he said. "Well, boys, if you have decided upon your plan, I guess I shall have to agree to it."

"I believe it will succeed," said Chester. "But at all events, we can't remain here inactive while that villain Robard is about his work."

"You're right there, Chester," said Hal. "Something must be done, and as there is no one else aware of this plot, I guess it is up to us."

"As I said before, you can count on me to the limit," said Uncle John.

"I'm counting on you, Uncle John," replied Chester. "I know you will do your part."

"Thanks," was the quiet response.

"Any more suggestions?" asked Chester.

There were none.

"What time is it?" asked Hal.

Chester glanced quickly at his watch.

"Great Scott!" he ejaculated. "Ten o'clock! I had no idea it was so late."

"Nor I," declared Uncle John.

"Time to get busy, then," said Hal.

"Right," Chester agreed. "We haven't a whole lot of time."

He gazed quickly about the room and then took his position at one side of the door, where he would not be seen by one entering the room. Hal and Uncle John also took their places.

"Everything ship-shape?" asked Chester.

"Guess so," replied Uncle John, somewhat nervously—he was not used to this kind of work, although each lad knew there was no question of his nerve and courage.

"All set," replied Hal quietly.

"Good!" said Chester. "Now for the disturbance. You fellows will have to help me out a little."

He raised his voice in a loud shout.

Hal and Uncle John followed suit.

"A terrible racket," said Chester, drawing a long breath a moment later. "It should raise the dead."

"It should," agreed Hal.

"But it didn't," said Chester. "Again. All together now, and keep it up."

Again the room rang with a horrible noise. Came footsteps running without.

Clair W. Hayes

CHAPTER XII

A FIGHT

"All ready now," called Chester in a hoarse whisper. "Here comes some one."

The others made no reply, but stood silently waiting.

The footsteps paused just outside the door.

"What's the matter in there?" asked a voice.

Chester made no reply; instead, he raised his voice in another blood-curdling shout.

The man outside wasted no more time in parley. Evidently he believed there was something serious the matter within. A key grated in the lock and the door swung inward.

Chester held himself tense—ready to spring upon the man the moment he should come within reach. Just inside the door the man paused and again sought to determine the cause of the commotion.

"What on earth is the matter in here?" he demanded loudly.

Seeking to help matters along, Hal gave vent to a sepulchral groan.

"Somebody must be sick," muttered the man to himself, and advanced into the room, casting discretion to the winds. One, two, three forward steps he took, and then whirled suddenly as Chester's hands closed about his throat from behind.

Now the Austrian was a big man, and in spite of Chester's strength, the lad realized in a moment that he was no match for his opponent.

"Quick, Hal, while I am able to hold him," he panted.

Hal wasted no time in words, for he realized it was time for action. He sprang from his place of concealment and darted toward the door, calling over his shoulder to Uncle John:

"Lend Chester a hand!"

But even as Hal would have darted through the door, the Austrian succeeded in freeing himself of Chester's hold, and hurling the lad from him with a swift backward kick, he turned just in time to encounter Hal.

Hal's right fist shot out sharply, and the Austrian staggered back as the blow caught him upon the point of the chin. But the blow had been delivered too quickly to have the desired effect, and the Austrian recovered himself in a moment, and, crouching low, advanced upon Hal. At the same time he raised his voice in a call for help.

"We'll have to dispose of this fellow pretty quick or it's all off," said Hal to the others. "Jump him from behind, Chester, while I keep him occupied here."

Chester needed no urging. He stepped aside quickly, and then jumped behind the Austrian, before the latter had time to back into a corner, had such been his intention. Uncle John circled about a bit and moved on him from the other side.

The Austrian took a quick look at his foes, threatening him from three sides. He realized he was no match for all, and his thoughts turned to escape. There was just one way by which he could get away—through the door by which he had entered the room—and this would give the prisoners a chance to make a break for liberty.

Hal struck out savagely with his right fist, and the Austrian hesitated no longer. With a quick backward leap, he passed from the room, making no effort to close the door behind him.

"After him!" cried Hal, also jumping forward.

The Austrian turned and took to his heels, and Hal, Chester and Uncle John gave chase. Down the hall ran the man, with Hal but a few paces behind him.

And then, suddenly, the Austrian turned in his tracks. Hal was quite unprepared for this maneuver, and before he could check himself, he had bumped squarely into his opponent, who seized him in close embrace. The man's hands closed about the boy's throat, and Hal gasped for breath.

Chester and Uncle John, seeing Hal's predicament, charged forward with a shout; and then the reason that the Austrian had turned to give battle became apparent.

A second and a third figure stepped around the two who were struggling in the center of the hall, and faced Uncle

John and Chester. One held a drawn revolver and the other was in the act of drawing a weapon.

It was no time to hesitate, and Chester realized it.

"Come on!" he cried, and leaped forward.

There came a flash and a loud report; but Chester was unwounded. He had stooped at the moment the man's hand pressed the trigger, and now came up beneath the other's guard. Before the latter could fire again, Chester drove him back with a hard right-handed blow to the jaw. The man uttered a low imprecation and at that instant Chester's left fist reached his opponent's stomach. The latter doubled up like a knife, and his revolver fell to the floor with a clatter.

Chester stooped quickly and his hand found the weapon. As he straightened up again, his eyes unconsciously took in the scene about him. He saw Hal make a last futile effort to free himself from the grasp of the first Austrian, and then fall to the floor with the man on top of him; and he saw Uncle John crumple up as a flash of flame came from the revolver of the third Austrian.

Chester gave a cry, and turning his newly acquired weapon in the direction of the man who had just fired at Uncle John, he pulled the trigger almost without taking aim. There came a cry, and the latter threw up his arms and fell to the floor. At the same moment the first Austrian rose from above Hal's prostrate form, and his revolver and Chester's spoke simultaneously. Chester felt a sharp tinge in his left arm and realized that he was not seriously hurt. He dropped quickly to the floor, even as the Austrian's revolver spoke again.

A bullet whizzed over his head. Chester now took deliberate aim and fired. The Austrian's weapon fell to the floor with a clatter, the man himself staggered and tried to retain his feet. He reeled forward toward Chester and then, just as the boy would have pressed the trigger again, collapsed almost at the lad's feet.

"I guess that settles the whole lot of you," Chester muttered to himself.

He ran quickly to where Hal lay and raised his chum's head to his knee. Hal made no move. Chester laid his hand over Hal's heart, and drew a breath of relief as he felt a faint beating. He stroked his friend's head, and rubbed his hands, and presently was rewarded by a sigh of returning consciousness.

Then Hal opened his eyes.

"Wow! A terrible dream I just had, Chester," he said.

Chester smiled in spite of himself.

"It came almost being your last dream," he replied quietly.

Without waiting for a reply, he laid Hal gently down again and hurried to Uncle John. The latter raised himself on one elbow even as Chester bent down beside him.

"Careless of me to get in the way of a bullet like that," he said with a faint smile. "I'll know better next time."

"Where are you hit, sir?" asked Chester anxiously.

"Caught me in the left side, some place," replied Uncle John, and with Chester's aid, got to his feet.

Chester made a quick examination.

"Lucky, sir. Just a flesh wound," he said. "I'll have it fixed up in a jiffy."

Making a bandage of his handkerchief, he soon had the wound tied up as well as could be done under the circumstances. Then the lad lent Hal a hand as the latter staggered to his feet.

"How do you feel?" asked Chester.

"Well, I don't feel very chipper, and that's a fact," replied Hal with a grimace. "That fellow had powerfully strong fingers."

"I guess we are lucky at that," remarked Chester.

"Lucky?" exclaimed Uncle John. "I'd like to know how you make that out, and me with a bullet hole in my side."

"Why," Chester explained, "the best we figured on was for one of us to get away, and now we are all at liberty."

"Perhaps we are," said Uncle John dryly. "I'll feel a whole lot safer when I once get outside of this house."

"Then we had better be moving," said Hal. "Come on."

He led the way to the end of the hall and into the room beyond.

"I guess we can get out this way," he said.

He examined a window at the far end of the room.

"Quite a drop down there," he said, "but I guess it can be done."

Clair W. Hayes

Chester and Uncle John also surveyed the distance to the ground.

"It's got to be done," said Uncle John. "I'll go first, if you don't mind."

"Go ahead, sir," said Hal.

Uncle John climbed to the sill, and then lowered himself until he hung by his hands.

"Here I go," he said.

He dropped.

"He's safe enough," said Chester, peering down, as Uncle John got to his feet and brushed himself off. "You next, Hal."

Hal climbed into the sill, lowered himself and dropped.

"All right," he called up to Chester.

Chester climbed to the sill.

"Here I come," he called; and just as he was about to lower himself a figure dashed suddenly into the room and seized him by the leg.

Chester gave vent to a cry of vexation.

"Hey," he called to Hal and Uncle John, "one of the big Austrians has grabbed me by the leg."

"Kick him in the face," cried Hal, dancing excitedly about, and making vain attempts to jump up so he could reach the sill.

Chester attempted to follow Hal's advice, but it was no use. Slowly he was dragged back through the window, and landed on the floor with a thud. When he was able to get to his feet, he faced a revolver held in a steady hand. He was caught and he knew it.

"He's got me, Hal," he shouted. "Hurry! Never mind me! Give the warning!"

For a single moment Hal hesitated after hearing Chester's voice. Then he took Uncle John by the arm.

"Chester is right," he muttered hoarsely. "Come on, sir, or we shall be captured, too."

Uncle John seemed about to protest, but Hal led him down the street at a rapid gait.

"What is one to many?" he asked.

CHAPTER XIII

CHESTER MISSES A CHANCE

Chester surveyed his captor with a slight smile on his face, although the bitterness of disappointment had touched his heart.

"Well, you've got me," he said quietly. "Now what are you going to do with me?"

The Austrian returned his look with a sour scowl.

"That is not for me to decide," he said. "Come with me."

He waved his revolver in the general direction of the door, and Chester walked out of the room. The Austrian followed closely, keeping his revolver close to the back of the lad's head. Evidently he had decided to take no further chances with him.

Chester smiled faintly to himself.

"Guess he'll hang on to me pretty tight this time," he muttered.

A moment later he found himself back in the same room the

three had been locked in when first brought to the house. The lad threw himself down dejectedly when the captor left the room and locked the door behind him.

"Well, I'm in for it now," he told himself. "Hal and Uncle John will warn the Italian general in time, and when Robard fails in his plot he'll come back to deal with me. I hope I am able to give a good account of myself. However, a fellow can never tell what is going to happen, so in order to be prepared, I'll try and get a little sleep."

He lay down and closed his eyes; and in spite of the seriousness of his situation, and the hard floor upon which he lay, he was soon asleep.

Meanwhile, Hal and Uncle John made all haste toward the headquarters of the Italian general staff, which at the moment were in Venice. It took Hal some moments to convince several subordinate officers that it was essential he see the commander himself, but after some explanations the lad, accompanied by Uncle John, was ushered into the presence of the general.

Hal laid bare the details of the plot in a few words, and the Italian commander eyed him incredulously.

"How am I to know you are telling the truth?" he demanded.

"For one reason, because I don't lie," replied Hal. "Besides, if you doubt me, sir, it would be well to be on the safe side, anyhow. It can do no harm to take the necessary precautions."

"What you say is true," replied the general.

"A wire to General Ferrari might tell you we are to be relied upon," continued Hal. "We were so fortunate as to be of some slight service to him recently."

The Italian commander glanced at his watch.

"It is best to be on the safe side," he said. "I shall take the necessary precautions, meanwhile wiring to General Ferrari, as you suggest. In the meantime, I fear I shall have to detain you, at least, until I receive a reply to my wire."

"But, sir," Hal protested, "I would like to go back and find my friend."

"I cannot permit that," was the reply. "How do I know that you are not spies yourselves and have concocted this story for some reason of your own—a reason that precautions I might take against the plot you have outlined might throw my troops into more serious difficulties? No, I shall keep you under guard. That is final."

Hal realized the futility of further protest and subsided. Not so Uncle John.

"This is an outrage, sir," he exploded. "I repeat, this is an outrage. Here we are, three of us, who have gone out of our way, to do the Italian army a service, and the best we get is trouble, fights and insults. I—"

The Italian commander raised a hand.

"I trust that you are telling the truth," he said turning to Hal, and ignoring Uncle John. "But I must make sure. You say you are a soldier. You can appreciate my position."

Hal nodded affirmatively. But Uncle John refused to be appeased.

"I think you are a lot of savages," he declared. "I wish the Austrians would blow up your whole army and drop bombs on every spot in the country. I'd help 'em do it if I had a good chance. I wouldn't turn my hand over to help you again."

The commander began to grow angry, and Hal realized it.

"That's enough, Uncle John," he remonstrated. "You'll get us in worse trouble than ever if you are not careful."

"Worse?" exclaimed Uncle John. "What can be worse than being in the same room with a bunch like this? I—"

Again the Italian commander raised a hand.

"Enough!" he said sharply. "I am convinced you have come here for no good. I shall send the wire I promised, but I am confident of the reply I shall receive. Orderly!"

An orderly approached.

"Keep these fellows safe," said the general.

"At least, sir, you will still take the precautions," said Hal.

The general hesitated a moment.

"Yes," he said finally, "you may at least have the satisfaction of knowing you have caused me to change my plans. All precautions shall be taken."

Hal and Uncle John were led away.

"I wonder what they have done with Chester?" said Uncle John.

"Whatever they have done will not be a circumstance to what they will do when Robard's plot fails," replied Hal. "That's why I was anxious not to antagonize the general. If the wire goes through we will possibly be in time to save him, if not—"

He broke off with a shrug.

"You mean—" began Uncle John.

"I don't know just what I mean," replied Hal. "I'm afraid. That's all."

Both lapsed into silence.

When Chester opened his eyes in his improvised prison the evil face of Robard bent over him. Chester sat up, stretched and then rose to his feet.

"Hello," he said. "Back again, I see."

Robard scowled fiercely, but made no reply.

"Well, did you blow up the whole Italian army?" asked Chester with a pleasant smile.

Robard stretched out a hand suddenly and seized Chester by the wrist and with his other hand struck the lad heavily in the face. Chester reeled back, but, recovering, promptly sent his right first into Robard's face.

The lad thought for a moment of following up his advantage and attempting to escape, but before he could act, Robard whipped out a revolver and covered him.

"Stand back!" he ordered.

Chester stood still.

"I've a notion to kill you right here," cried the Austrian furiously. "What do you mean by hitting me?"

"What do you mean by hitting me?" demanded Chester.

"You young American upstart!" shouted the enraged Austrian. "I'll—"

"I wouldn't if I were you," said Chester calmly, as Robard raised a heavy fist. "You may be able to fight with a gun or a knife, but don't come at me with your fists or I'll spank you."

If Chester's object had been to enrage the Austrian he had succeeded. Robard cast discretion to the winds, and, lowering his revolver, struck at the lad.

It was the chance for which Chester had been waiting and hoping.

He ducked under the heavy blow, and instead of returning it, he kicked out with his left foot. His aim was true and Robard's revolver fell to the floor with a clatter. Chester pounced on it, beating the Austrian by the fraction of a second. A moment later the Austrian struck him a heavy blow on the side of the face.

Chester became suddenly very angry—not furiously and excitedly so, but his temper blazed up and his anger was quiet and deadly. Calmly he blocked a second blow from his opponent and took the time to put the revolver hastily in his pocket.

"Now," he said, "I am going to give you a first class licking. I didn't take boxing lessons for nothing, and if you have anything to say when I get through I'll be willing to listen."

At that moment the Austrian rushed. Chester side-stepped neatly, and his left fist crashed to the side of the Austrian's jaw as the latter brushed past. Before Robard could turn, Chester planted his right fist upon the back of the other's neck, sending him staggering.

Then he waited for Robard to come at him again.

Turning, Robard advanced more cautiously this time. Chester feinted with his right, and sent his left to Robard's nose. Blood flowed. Chester danced about the big Austrian, raining blows upon him almost at will.

"Take that, and that, and that," he said gleefully, skipping first this way and then that, skillfully evading the heavy blows launched wildly by Robard.

This continued for perhaps five minutes, and then Chester grew tired.

"Well, we'll end it now," he told the Austrian with a smile. "Watch, here comes the finish."

He stiffened a bit, took a backward step, then danced suddenly forward. He feinted with dazzling rapidity once, twice, three times, and then, his opponent completely bewildered, planted his right fist squarely upon the point of Robard's chin. Robard staggered back, but a second terrific blow, delivered to the stomach, brought him forward again, and Chester straightened him up with another terrific drive to the point of the chin.

The lad stepped back and dropped his hands, watching the big Austrian with a smile on his face.

Clear across the room the man staggered and then crumpled up in a heap.

"That settles him," said Chester. "Now to get out of here."

He turned toward the door, and stopped, a cry of dismay on his lips.

In the doorway stood three figures. As Chester turned, one of them advanced toward him.

"You did a pretty job," he said, eyeing the lad appreciatively, "and we are glad to have seen it. But, we cannot let you escape."

Chester groaned and sat down.

"There're too many of them," he said to himself. "So near and yet so far. If I hadn't let my temper get the best of me I would have been safely out of here. I'll never waste another second on an Austrian. This is what I get for not shooting him like a dog, and using my fists on him, like I would on a gentleman. Never again."

CHAPTER XIV

THE AMBASSADOR AGAIN

While Hal, Chester and Uncle John were having their troubles with members of the Austrian diplomatic corps on Italian soil, the Italian army itself already had taken the field against the enemy. War having been declared, the Italian general staff had wasted no time.

Along the Austrian frontier, at the head of the Adriatic, clear north to the Swiss border, the troops of King Emmanuel had intrenched themselves against a possible attack of the foe; big guns even now were roaring and raining the messengers of death upon the fortified positions of the Austrians in their front.

Skirmishes between isolated forces of the two armies, some of which reached the proportions of real battles, had taken place, and upon the southern border some slight success already had crowned the efforts of the Italian troops.

The Italian fleet had been set in motion; giant battleships and other vessels of war had joined other craft of the quadruple entente in an effective blockade of Austrian ports in the Adriatic; and the Austrians were keeping well behind the shelter of their own mines.

In one or two cases they had ventured forth to give battle, but each expedition of this nature had resulted disastrously—at the bottom of the sea. Apparently, now, they had given up attempts to run the blockade and were content to lie snug in their well-fortified harbors, even as their German allies were doing in their ports.

Several Austrian aircraft had left their bases and flown over Genoa, dropping bombs, killing and wounding a score of non-combatants, but doing little damage to fortified positions or to munition plants and provision camps, which were presumed to be their goal. Also several had been brought to earth by the accurate fire from the anti-air craft guns of the Italians.

Unlike England, France, Russia and Belgium, Italy entered the war prepared. She was not taken by surprise, as had been her allies. She went into the war with her eyes open and a full realization of her responsibilities. Also mobilization had been completed before she had finally decided to take the plunge into the maelstrom. Again, she was better prepared than her allies for the reason that she had recently emerged from a successful struggle against the Turks in Tripoli and her army was an army of veterans.

There was no doubt that Italy would be the first to take the offensive. The question was, where would she strike? It was an established fact that she would not await the attacks of the Austrians, but where would she deliver her first blow? Would it be by sea, hurling her fleet upon the enemy's base across the Adriatic? Would it be across the southern boundary of Austria, or would it be farther north—through the Alps?

There was little to choose between the latter methods; but the first was given little thought. It was well known that the

Clair W. Hayes

Austrians had mined the Adriatic thoroughly near their ports, and to attempt an expedition there threatened destruction for the attackers.

An advance through the Alps also presented its difficulties. In spite of the fact that the weather was still warm, it was anything but warm in the mountain fastnesses. True, a passage of the Alps had been forced before now—one by the Carthaginian General Hannibal in the middle ages, and again by Napoleon. But it was still a desperate undertaking.

The world waited to see.

Chester Crawford, still in the hands of his captors, took no thought of these things now. His one absorbing thought at the moment was of hitting upon some plan whereby he could elude his guards and make his escape. At the same time, he realized that he had a hard problem before him; for now that he had almost made his get-away twice, he knew he would be guarded with more vigilance than before. Still, he determined to bide his time and take advantage of the first opportunity that presented itself.

The two Austrians who had arrived in time to prevent his escape after his tussle with Robard now stood guard over the lad, waiting for Robard to return to consciousness. Presently the fallen man stirred, rolled over, gasped a bit, and sat up. He gazed about and took in his surroundings. An ugly look passed over his face as his eyes fell upon Chester.

"I'll get even with you for this," he said harshly, as he scrambled to his feet.

"Oh, I don't know," returned Chester with a smile. "I might only increase my indebtedness the next time we meet."

The Austrian took a threatening step forward. Chester did not flinch and the man paused and dropped the arm he had raised.

"I'll wait till we get to Vienna, and then I'll guarantee to make you whine for mercy," growled Robard.

"We shall see," said Chester.

Robard turned to his men.

"We'll go at once," he said.

"By the way," interrupted Chester, "what has happened to the ambassador?"

Robard gave a start, and looked quickly at his two men, who had turned at Chester's words.

"You'll find him in the next room, I think," said Chester, pointing.

"Shut up!" commanded Robard, again taking a step forward.

Chester smiled and stepped back a bit.

"Where you shot him," he continued pleasantly.

With a cry Robard leaped upon him. Chester struck out quickly with both fists, one after the other, and the Austrian staggered back. Chester turned to the others.

"What I say is true," he said quietly, as he noted the look of uncertainty on their faces. "You can easily tell by investigating."

"It's a lie!" shouted Robard.

The men hesitated.

"Look and see," said Chester.

"The boy is right," said one of them. "I'll look."

He stepped toward the door.

"Stand where you are!" cried Robard.

He moved upon the other and clenched his fists. The man gazed at him a moment without a word; then, suddenly, he seized his superior by the arms and held him as though he had been in a vise.

"You have a look, Fritz," he said to his companion. "I'll hold him safe enough."

The latter wasted no time. He hurried from the room.

"You'll pay for this!" screamed Robard.

"Perhaps," said his subordinate, "but I believe the boy has told the truth. I never did trust you, with your shifty eyes."

At that moment the third man came back into the room, dragging a heavy body after him.

"The ambassador!" cried the other.

"You see, I was right," said Chester.

The ambassador was unconscious still, although it was hours after he had been wounded.

"He's alive," said one of the Austrians, after an examination.

"Get some water," commanded the other.

At this moment Robard took a step forward, and seemed about to wrench himself free from his captor's arms.

"If you gentlemen will allow me," said Chester, "I shall make a suggestion that may save us all time and bother."

"Well?" demanded one of the men.

"If you'll give me the gun you deprived me of," said the boy, "I'll give my word to hold our friend here safe until the ambassador is brought back to consciousness. Also, I give my word not to attempt to escape."

The others eyed him closely for a brief moment.

"All right," said the man who had gone after the ambassador. "Here." He passed over his automatic.

Chester took it and covered Robard.

"You can release him now," he said to the big Austrian's captor. "He'll make no break while I have him covered. He knows me too well by this time, don't you, Robard?"

The latter's reply was a low growl.

The other Austrian released his hold, and stood back. For an instant it seemed that Robard would spring forward and give battle to all three, but as Chester's revolver covered him steadily, he changed his mind and stood still.

Immediately the others began the work of reviving the

ambassador, and five minutes later their efforts were rewarded. The ambassador moaned feebly, and a few seconds later sat up. His eyes fell on Robard, and he jumped quickly to his feet.

"So!" he exclaimed. "Guard him carefully, boy. He's a dangerous man."

"I'll guard him," replied Chester briefly.

Suddenly the Austrian smote himself on the breast.

"The plot!" he cried. "Robard's plot!"

"Has failed," interrupted Chester. Then noticing the look of surprise on the ambassador's face, he explained.

"We overheard the conversation in the room where we were locked, sir. My friends managed to escape and give the warning. The plot has failed. Robard told me as much."

"I'm glad," said the ambassador simply. "And now, what am I to do with you?"

"Let me go, sir," was the lad's reply.

The ambassador considered the matter.

"I'll tell you," he said at length, "I would like for you to go to Vienna with me and substantiate my story to the emperor. You will say that my story should need no proof, as I am the ambassador, but Robard has influential friends there. He would easily discredit the stories of these two men here. With you it would be different. Will you go?"

"I would rather not, sir," replied Chester quietly.

"I must insist," urged the ambassador.

For some reason that Chester was never afterwards able to explain to himself, he suddenly grew terribly angry.

"No, I won't go!" he shouted, and waved a fist in the very face of the ambassador.

The latter looked at him in amazement; then took his decision.

"You shall go anyhow," he said softly. "Seize him, men!"

CHAPTER XV

INTO AUSTRIA

"Any time," said the ambassador gently, "that you are ready to give me your parole, I shall have your bonds removed."

"I wouldn't give my parole to you or any other of your kind," declared Chester grimly.

"I'm sorry you feel that way about it," declared the ambassador, with a deprecating gesture. "I assure you, I shall see that you are given safe conduct back to Italy. But in the meantime, I can take no chances upon your escaping."

"Do as you please," said Chester.

Again a captive, Chester left Venice.

In a first class compartment of the special train that was bearing the Austrian ambassador and his staff rapidly toward Trieste was also Chester, nursing a sore head, the result of trying to vanquish the ambassador and the two other Austrians when the diplomat had ordered him seized. The lad put up such a battle that one of his opponents had found it necessary to tap him gently on top of the head with the butt of his revolver. That had settled the argument, and when

Chester returned to consciousness he was aboard the special train, bound, and seated across from the ambassador.

"Sorry we had to give you that crack on the head," the ambassador continued, "but you wouldn't behave without it. Does it pain you much?"

"Not so much as the fact that you are a race lacking in all sense of gratitude," replied Chester. "I wish now I had let you lie where you were. The next time I shall keep my mouth shut, you can bet on that."

"Well, anyhow, here you are," said the ambassador, "and I promise that you shall remain with me until I see the emperor in Vienna, if I have to drug you. After that, I promise you safe conduct to the Italian border. Come, why not be sensible?"

But Chester was in no mood to be sensible, and there is little wonder. Twice he had almost regained his liberty, and a third time, after he had come to the assistance of the ambassador, he felt certain he would be set free. He was far from cheerful now.

"We are now in Austria," said the ambassador, an hour later.

"It won't be so long before it will be Italy, I guess," said Chester, with something like a sneer in his voice.

"Come, come, my friend," said the ambassador. "Don't let your feelings run away with you. You are simply talking to hear yourself talk."

"Don't you believe it," declared Chester. "I know what I am talking about. Say! You fellows don't think you can whip the world, do you?"

"Well, we seem to have been whipping a pretty good part of it," replied the ambassador sententiously.

"That's it! That's it!" cried Chester. "That's your Teutonic air of conquerors. Don't forget that some of these days, however, you will be sorry for all this trouble and bloodshed you have caused."

"We have caused?" echoed the ambassador. "You mean that England has caused."

"No, I don't mean England," replied Chester.

"Why," exclaimed the ambassador, "if it had not been for England, this war would never have happened."

Chester looked at the ambassador sharply for a moment.

"Good night," he said at last, and fell back in his seat.

It was dusk when the train pulled into Trieste, and the party alighted.

"We shall spend the night here," the ambassador decided. "I have some work to do."

"One place suits me as well as another, if I have to stay in this kind of a country," said Chester.

At a hotel where they were driven in a taxi, Chester was locked in a room on the fifth floor. It was a handsomely appointed room, and Chester would have been content to spend the night there had he been in other circumstances. But right now he wasn't content to spend the night in Austria, no matter how well he was treated.

"I want to get out of this country," he told himself repeatedly. "I guess it's a good enough country, so far as it goes, but I can plainly see it's no place for me."

Left alone, Chester made a tour of inspection. The door was heavily barred. He looked out the window.

"A long way to the ground," he muttered.

There was no other means of egress.

"Looks like I was safe enough," he muttered.

Again he examined the window carefully. A slight whistle escaped him.

"A little risky," he told himself, "but I believe it can be done."

He walked to the door, laid his ear against it and listened intently. No sound came from without.

"Well," he said, straightening up, "if I am going to do it, the sooner I get busy the better."

Quickly he stripped the covering from the bed, and with his knife slit it lengthwise. Each strip he tied to another, until he had a strong improvised rope. He stretched it out on the floor, and measured it carefully with his eye. Then he again walked to the window and peered out.

"Pretty close," he muttered, "but I believe it will reach. The trouble is some one in one of the rooms below is liable to see me."

Now he pushed the bed close to the window, and securely

knotted one end of his improvised rope to the heavy iron bars. Then he walked across the room to the door again and listened.

It was now dark outside and Chester realized that he could not have a better moment for his desperate attempt. Quickly he recrossed the room, and dropped the other end of the rope out the window. He glanced down.

"O.K.," he said. "Here goes."

He leaped quickly to the sill, and a moment later was lowering himself hand over hand. And at length he came to the end of the rope.

The ground was still far below him, but Chester had not figured the rope would reach to the ground. Clinging tightly to the rope, he gazed quickly about.

He was now even with the window on the third floor, and he succeeded by clever work in getting a foothold on the sill; and, still clinging to the rope, he stood erect. Inside, Chester saw the figure of a man. Inadvertently, the lad's foot crashed against the window pane, shattering the glass. There was a crash, followed by a guttural exclamation from inside the room.

"I've got to move now!" exclaimed the lad.

Taking a firm hold on the rope, he swung himself outward, giving his flight through space an added impetus by pushing with his right foot. He went sailing through the air, even as a pistol shot rang out behind him.

Chester had calculated truly. Headfirst he crashed among the branches of a tree, at the far side of the walk. Instantly he released his hold upon the rope and was safe in the tree.

"I thought I could do it," he muttered. "Now to get down before some of these fellows get after me."

Rapidly he made his descent, and a few moments later stood upon the sidewalk, unhurt. For a moment he paused to gain a much-needed breath, and then, turning, he stalked quickly away. And as he did so there came cries from within the hotel, and men rushed out and after him.

Chester took to his heels.

"I don't know whether they saw me on the street or not," he told himself, "but the safest place for me is a long way from that hotel."

He doubled around several corners, and at last, as he turned into a more traveled street, he slowed down to a walk. He drew a long breath.

"Guess I have shaken them," he said. "Now, if I only knew where I was, I might manage to get out of here. Guess I had better pick one direction and keep going that way. I'll trust to luck that it is either north or west."

He turned down the next street and set out resolutely, having determined in his mind to stick to the direction he had selected. Fortunately, although the lad could not be sure of it, he was heading northward, where, eventually, he would reach the Italian frontier, although it was much further away than was the western border.

Chester walked along for an hour without even being challenged.

Clair W. Hayes

"Funny, too," he muttered. "It's a wonder every street corner doesn't spout soldiers and police at me. I must be getting to be rather a lucky young man."

He had now reached a less thickly populated district. There were few pedestrians upon the streets, houses became farther and farther apart. An occasional automobile passed him, but no attention was paid to the hurrying figure.

Chester slowed down a trifle as he made out a form approaching. As it drew closer Chester noticed it was a uniformed figure. He drew a deep breath.

"Looks like there was liable to be something doing here," he muttered.

He continued his way. The officer, for such Chester perceived the man to be, drew closer. As Chester would have passed him, he suddenly stopped in his tracks, and commanded:

"Halt!"

Chester did so.

"Who are you?" demanded the man, "and where are you going?"

To Chester's great relief, he spoke in German, and the lad replied in the same language, which he spoke without an accent.

"I am on an errand for the ambassador, sir. A prisoner has recently escaped, and I am bearing word to the outposts to be on the watch for him."

"Hm-m-m," muttered the officer. "Why didn't the ambassador make use of the wireless 'phone?"

"I don't know, sir," replied Chester.

The officer laid a heavy hand on the lad's arm, and peered into his face in the dim light. Then the hand tightened.

"You are no German!" was his quiet comment. "You are probably a spy. You are my prisoner!"

Chester's heart sank.

Clair W. Hayes

CHAPTER XVI

A FRIEND IN NEED

Many thoughts ran through Chester's head as he stood there for a brief moment with the hand of the man who had accosted him on his shoulder. He thought of flight and he thought of fight, but most of all he thought of the ill fortune he had encountered in the past few days.

"This is the limit," he told himself ruefully. Aloud he said: "You are mistaken, sir."

"No, I'm not mistaken," returned the officer, "and I suppose most would take you at your word. You speak German without an accent, but your face betrays you. At a guess, I would say you are English."

"You are wrong," declared Chester.

"Nevertheless, I shall have to ask you to accompany me," said the officer.

For a moment Chester hesitated; he was tempted to leap upon his captor and make a fight for it, but he had hesitated too long now. The officer produced a revolver, which he held carelessly in his right hand.

"I have a little persuader here, in case you should think of disobeying my order," he said quietly.

"Oh, all right," said Chester. "I'll go along."

"I thought you would," replied his captor, with a smile.

He motioned for Chester to walk on ahead of him, which the boy did, the while grumbling to himself.

"I should have run when I saw him coming," he muttered.

There was little doubt in Chester's mind now that he was due for his trip to Vienna with the ambassador. After that, in view of his attempt to escape, he wasn't sure what might happen, for he believed the ambassador would recall his offer of a safe conduct after this.

"Yes, it looks like Vienna to me," he told himself.

And so it probably would have been but for one thing—or rather, for one person; and Chester had no more idea of seeing him than he had of encountering Hal at the next cross street.

As the two walked along, Chester slightly in front, his captor following him closely with drawn revolver, a figure left the shadow of a nearby building, and with a whistle of amazement, crept silently in their wake.

"Well! Well!" muttered this figure to himself. "What do you think of that? I can't stand for this. I'm liable to get killed or hurt, but I've just got to take a hand."

As Chester and his captor turned into another street and disappeared from sight, the man broke into a run, stepping lightly on his toes. When he rounded the corner he was only a few feet behind the other two. Silently as a cat, he closed up the distance, drawing a weapon from his pocket as he ran.

He took the revolver by the barrel, and with a sudden leap, sprang upon the officer who had captured Chester. A quick blow and the officer staggered. He seemed about to cry out, but even as he opened his mouth, the newcomer repeated the blow and the man fell to the sidewalk without a word.

"It's all right, Chester," said the newcomer.

Chester, who had stood as if petrified during the struggle— he was so surprised at this sudden and unexpected aid— uttered an exclamation of surprise.

"Who are you?" he asked, in vain trying to pierce the darkness with his eyes.

The stranger chuckled.

"You don't know, eh?" he asked.

Again Chester peered at him intently. It was so dark he could not make out the man's features, but there was something very familiar about the short, rotund figure that stood before him.

"By Jove!" cried the lad at last. "It is—it can't be—yes, it must be—"

"Anthony Stubbs, war correspondent of the New York *Gazette*, sir, and very much at your service," came the now well-known voice.

Chester sprang forward and seized the extended hand.

"And what in the name of all that's wonderful are you doing here?" he asked in amazement.

"Getting some red-hot news for the New York *Gazette*," was Stubbs' laconic response. "You are liable to find me most any place. As I told you before, there is no place a newspaper man cannot go. Now, what's all this mess I find you in?"

Chester explained and Stubbs listened attentively.

"Hm-m-m," he said, when the lad had concluded, "I guess the best thing for you to do is to hop back into Italy as fast as the law allows."

"My idea," said Chester dryly. "The trouble is it's a pretty long hop, and in the next place the Austrian law doesn't allow it."

"That's so," agreed Stubbs. "However, you just leave these little things to Anthony. He'll get you through or the New York *Gazette* will lose its best man."

"Well, I hope the *Gazette* doesn't lose him," said Chester; "but I would like to get back into civilization."

"Civilization?" echoed the little man. "And what do you call this? Let one of these uniformed gentleman on this side of the border hear you say that and you won't ever get any place except under the sod. This, take the Austrian word for it, is the last word in civilization. Therefore, what you mean is that you want to get out of civilization."

"Whichever way suits you," agreed Chester.

"All right. Then you come with me. It's time to be moving,

anyhow. This fellow is getting about ready to get up and there is no use of our being here to greet him when he opens his eyes. Let's go."

He led the way back toward the heart of the city and Chester followed, though not without a protest.

"What's the use of going back there?" he wanted to know. "That's the place I have been trying to get away from."

"Now listen here, young man," said Stubbs, "you didn't have much luck getting away by yourself, did you?"

"No," replied Chester, "but—"

"And you won't have any better now, if you don't do as I say," declared Stubbs. "But I'll tell you. I am leaving here myself in the morning. I am going to Italy. I've dug up all the stuff I can get around here and now I'm going to have a look at the Italian army in action. If you wish, you can come along."

"Of course I'll come," said Chester. "That is, if they will let me."

"Oh, they'll let you, all right," replied Stubbs. "Say, I guess you don't know who I am! I'll tell you: I'm the war correspondent of the New York *Gazette*, and these fellows over here are glad to show me what favors they can. It doesn't do them any harm, and it might do them some good. See?"

"I see," agreed Chester briefly.

"All right, then. I'll take you to my lodgings and you can spend the night there with me. We'll leave early in the morning."

Chester followed the little man, though not without some misgivings.

Apparently Stubbs had not spoken without reason. Along the way they passed several officers, each of whom, after recognizing the war correspondent, gave him a formal military salute.

"You see," said Stubbs, "I am some pumpkins around these parts."

"So I see," replied Chester.

"Here is where we put up," said Stubbs presently, turning into a large and well-lighted hotel. "Put your best foot foremost now, and walk in like you owned the place. Can you swagger a bit?"

"Well, some," said Chester hesitatingly.

"So can I," said Stubbs, "which is the reason I get along so well. Follow me."

His usual manner—the one to which Chester had become accustomed when he had been with the little man in the French theater of war, left him as he entered the door, and he swaggered in like a true bravo. Chester threw out his shoulders and did likewise.

Straight up to the desk walked Stubbs, where a clerk came courteously forward to see what was desired.

"My friend here," said Stubbs, with a wave of his hand, "will share my room to-night. Have us called at six o'clock and send a man to help me with my things at that hour. Understand?"

"Yes, Herr Stubbs," replied the clerk, rubbing his hands together, though why Chester did not know. "It shall be done."

"All right," said Stubbs. "My key!"

The clerk hastened to get it.

"Now that's the way to get by in this benighted land," said Stubbs to Chester as they made their way to the little man's room. "Make 'em think you own the place. It never hurts anything."

"So I see," said Chester dryly. "Now, about the morning. How do we get out of this country?"

"Simple," said Stubbs. "We take an automobile from here to a little town called Gorz, to the north. And then we circle around the little neck of Italy to Trent, again in Austria. Of course there are quicker ways out, but I have made these arrangements already and it would look suspicious to change now. Until we get to Trent there will be no trouble. There we shall have to do a little figuring, but the best way is this: I have a safe conduct, given me by the Austrian commander here. It will pass me into Italy. What I shall do is give it to you and you can cross the border."

"But you—" began Chester.

"I'm coming to that. They will stop me, of course. Then I'll raise a holler. I'll demand that they wire the commander here and give a description of me, saying I have lost my papers. They will identify me, all right, because there are no more like me. A second safe conduct will come along and I'll move into Italy. Simple little thing, isn't it?"

"Quite simple—if it works," said Chester.

"Oh, it'll work all right!"

"I hope so," declared Chester.

"It's got to work," replied Stubbs. "I can't afford to have it fail. My paper will be expecting something out of Italy from me within a few days and I've got to be there to give it to them. Otherwise, I'm liable to be dismissed."

"I guess that won't happen," said Chester, with a smile.

"Not if I can help it," agreed Stubbs. "Now let's climb between the sheets."

Clair W. Hayes

CHAPTER XVII

BACK INTO ITALY

"Now here," said Stubbs, "are my papers. You just take them, and for the moment you will be Anthony Stubbs, war correspondent of the New York *Gazette*. You are a little young looking, so put on all the airs you can, for they'll think you must be awful good to have such a job."

Chester and the little war correspondent had left Trieste without trouble and had arrived in Trent without adventure of any kind. True to his word, Stubbs had arranged for Chester's departure with him and now the time for parting had come.

Chester took the papers Stubbs held out to him and thrust them into his pocket.

"And when will you be across?" he asked.

"Oh, I'll be there before the day is over," was the reply. "When you once get within the Italian lines, you demand to be taken to the nearest general commanding a division and explain matters to him. Then wait for me, if it is until to-morrow. I'll be there."

"All right," agreed Chester.

"I'll walk as far as the outposts with you," said Stubbs. "No, I won't either," on second thought. "I'll be wanting to get out myself directly and it wouldn't do for us to be seen together."

He held out his hand.

"Good-bye, and good luck," he said. "You just do as I tell you and you'll have no trouble. Remember, you are just as big as any of these fellows, and a whole lot bigger, if it comes to that."

Chester gripped the hand hard.

"Good-bye," he said, "and thanks."

The little man gazed after the boy as the latter strode away with shoulders squared and head held high.

"He'll do," he muttered to himself.

Chester disappeared, and Stubbs turned and strode in the opposite direction.

"Now for my holler—and my new papers," he told himself.

Chester was halted at the extreme Austrian front. He produced Stubbs' papers, which he gave the man without a word. Luckily, as Stubbs had explained, the safe conduct was simply made out to "Anthony Stubbs, war correspondent," without description.

The officer scanned the papers closely, looked Chester over from head to foot and seemed about to speak. Chester gazed at him sternly and the Austrian closed his lips without uttering a word. He shrugged his shoulders, summoned an orderly and commanded:

"Take a flag of truce and conduct this gentleman to the Italian lines."

Two hours later Chester was safe.

To the Italian officer who approached him, he demanded to be taken to the general commanding the division, and this was done without protest. Chester explained the circumstances to the general, and the latter believed him. He turned him over to an orderly, with instructions that he be taken care of; and in a tent of his own, Chester sat down to await the arrival of Stubbs.

Stubbs, after Chester had left him, immediately betook himself to the commander of the Austrian forces at this point. The latter received him, although he didn't know Stubbs from any one else.

"General," said Stubbs, "somebody stole my papers, among them a safe conduct to the Italian lines. I want to get there."

"No papers, no safe conduct," replied the general briefly.

This was what Stubbs had expected.

"Look here now, general," he said familiarly, "that's no way for you to talk. I want to get into Italy, and I had safe conduct from General Oberlatz at Trieste."

The Austrian commander got to his feet.

"I have told you, sir," he said, "that without papers you cannot leave our lines."

"I heard you," replied Stubbs, "but you don't seem to understand the answer to my being here. I've got to get into the Italian lines. You can't blame me. The fellow you want is the one who stole my papers; he's probably a spy."

"And you may be one, too," said the officer.

"Sure, I may be," said Stubbs; "only I'm not. Now, I'll tell you, you just push through a little wire to General Oberlatz and he'll straighten this thing out."

"Can't be done," replied the general.

"But it's got to be done," declared Stubbs. "I can't stay around here when I have orders to go elsewhere. I don't want to have to take this matter up with my friend, the archduke."

The Austrian commander looked up in surprise at this last remark.

"You know the archduke?" he questioned.

"Well, rather," said Stubbs. "He and I are pretty good friends."

"Then," said the general, "it would do no harm for you to appeal to him in person."

"You're right, there, general," declared Stubbs. "My friend, the archduke, would fix this thing up in a minute. The only trouble on that score is the matter of time. Time is precious, you know, general, and time presses."

"Fortunately for you," said the officer, "the archduke happens to be in the next room at this moment. If you will be seated, I shall call him."

Stubbs sat down abruptly. A slight whistle escaped him, though it did not carry to the general's ears.

"Good night!" muttered the little man to himself. "I've sure enough gone and done it this time."

But Stubbs didn't betray himself. To the general he said:

"The archduke here? By Jove! This is what I call luck. Have him come out and talk to me."

With a bow, the Austrian commander turned and passed from the room. The moment he crossed the threshold, Stubbs sprang to his feet and dashed to the door through which he had entered a few moments before.

"This," he said, as he came again into the open, "is no place for Anthony Stubbs."

He disappeared from within view of the general's quarters with amazing rapidity.

"Wasn't much use of me patting the archduke on the back," he told himself. "Never having seen me before, I guess he wouldn't have remembered me. I don't want to be shot."

Half a mile from the scene of his trouble, he entered a little restaurant and sat down to have something to eat and to figure out what he should do.

"This place is going to be too small to hold me," he said to himself over a second cup of coffee. "They'll have all the natives on my trail. I've got to get over the frontier some way. The question before me is how?"

He meditated for some moments, then rose, paid his check

and left the restaurant. In front of the door he stopped and looked toward the south, where, in the distance, he knew heavy Austrian patrols faced the Italian pickets only a few miles beyond.

"That's the way I want to go," he told himself. "So I may as well be starting in that direction."

He moved off.

Possibly half a mile from the utmost Austrian line he stopped and sat down. So far he had been unchallenged and now, as he sat there, a plan came to him. He took his revolver from his pocket and examined it.

"I'll try it," he said briefly to himself. "If Chester knew what I was about to do, he would be greatly surprised. But the thing is I am more afraid to stay here than I am to take this chance."

He arose and moved on. As he expected, probably five minutes later, a mounted officer came toward him. There was no one else near. He halted the correspondent.

"Where are you going?" he asked sharply.

"I'll tell you," was the reply. "I am a war correspondent and I am just looking about a bit. Am I going too far? If so, I shall turn back."

"Well, I can permit you to go no farther," said the Austrian, with a smile.

"Oh, all right," said Stubbs.

He drew a cigar from his pocket, bit off the end, struck a

match and lighted it. Then, with a start, he produced a second cigar.

"Beg pardon," he said. "Have a smoke?"

The Austrian signified that he would. Stubbs gave him the cigar and struck a second match. The Austrian leaned from his horse and put the cigar to the flame. At that moment Stubbs drew his revolver with his free hand and, dropping the match, seized the Austrian by the leg with the other. The latter came tumbling from his horse, and when he looked up, he gazed squarely into the mouth of Stubbs' revolver.

"Quiet," said the little man briefly. "I want you to change clothes with me."

The Austrian appeared about to protest, but changed his mind and signified his willingness to comply with the command.

"Stand off there and remove your clothes," ordered Stubbs, pointing.

The man obeyed, Stubbs the while keeping him covered with his revolver. The man's clothes removed, Stubbs approached him.

"I'll have to tie you up minus your outer garments," he told him. "I can't take any chances on you while I am donning your robes."

He tied him up in most approved fashion and then gagged him with his handkerchief.

"Just to keep you from giving an alarm," he said.

Rapidly he donned the Austrian's clothes and then walked over to his horse. This he mounted and turned the animal's head southward. He waved a hand at the Austrian.

"*Auf Wiedersehen*," he said, and rode away.

He kept as far as possible from the Austrian troops that patrolled the outposts and half an hour later was beyond the Austrian lines. Out of sight he halted and discarded the Austrian uniform he had drawn on over his civilian attire and then rode on more confidently.

And the little man welcomed a command that broke upon his ears a short time later:

"Halt!"

He drew rein. A soldier in Italian uniform advanced toward him.

"Thank the Lord," said the little man.

He drew a hand across a moist brow and gave a whistle of pure relief.

"No one will ever know how scared I was," he muttered. "Now to find Chester."

He turned to the soldier who had accosted him.

"Take me immediately to your commanding officer," he ordered.

CHAPTER XVIII

HAL AND UNCLE JOHN

While Chester and his old friend, Anthony Stubbs, war correspondent, are resting at ease for the moment with the Italian troops at the extreme northern front, it behooves us to go back and see what has happened to Hal and Uncle John.

When the two were led away from the headquarters of the Italian commander, under guard, Uncle John's rage had by no means subsided; but he cooled down somewhat after Hal had, to the best of his ability, attempted to show him the viewpoint of the general.

"It's a contemptible trick," Uncle John protested.

"Well, let it go at that, then," said Hal helplessly.

And Uncle John did.

Now the thoughts of the two turned to Chester, for both were greatly worried about him, and their anxiety increased as the long hours passed.

So darkness came, and they lay down to sleep. They were awake with the morning light and the first thought of each was whether any word had been received from the Italian commander in Rome.

And two hours after daylight they knew. An orderly entered and informed them that the commander desired their presence immediately. They followed him.

"Everything all right, general?" Hal greeted him, with a smile.

The Italian commander frowned.

"The answer to my wire will hardly gain you your freedom," he replied.

"What, sir?" demanded Hal, in great surprise.

"Exactly," replied the commander, this time smiling a little himself.

"What did General Ferrari say?" inquired Hal anxiously.

"Well, he didn't say anything," replied the Italian. "He is no longer in Rome, but has gone to the front. My wire did not reach him. Consequently, I shall have to turn you over to the civil authorities here for safe-keeping. I cannot be bothered with you."

Hal gazed at Uncle John in dismay.

"What did I tell you?" the latter broke out. "And you sided with him, too. Tried to show me where he was right, didn't you? Well, what do you think of him now?"

In spite of the seriousness of their situation, Hal was forced to smile at Uncle John's righteous wrath.

"It will turn out all right," he said quietly.

"I'm glad somebody thinks so," declared Uncle John. "I don't."

Hal addressed the commander:

"General, I can assure you that all we have said has been the truth. You will learn so in time. I, sir, have seen active service. I have fought with the Belgians, the British in France and the Russians in the eastern war zone."

"From your own accounts you must have had quite a time," said the Italian commander dryly. "Now, I may as well tell you that I do not believe a single word of your story and protests will avail you nothing. Were I to follow my own inclinations, I would order you both shot as spies within the hour. However, there is always a chance that my convictions may be wrong, which is the only thing that is saving you now. I shall wait until I have word from General Ferrari. Orderly!"

A subordinate entered.

"Turn these prisoners over to Colonel Brunoli. Colonel Brunoli," he continued, addressing Hal, "is the chief of police. I can guarantee that you will be safe in his keeping."

Hal would have protested, but the orderly signalled him to march out ahead, of him. Hal took Uncle John by the arm, and they left, but not before Uncle John had hurled a final remark over his shoulder to the Italian commander.

"You will hear of me again, sir," he thundered. "I'm an American citizen and we have an ambassador over in this benighted country. He'll warm things up for you when he learns of this outrage."

"March!" commanded the orderly and Uncle John heeded the order.

Before an imposing building a short distance away, the orderly called a halt and then motioned them up the short flight of steps. Through a long hall they were marched and into a room at the far end. Here a man in uniform with much lace and gold facings sat at a large desk. Hal didn't need to be told that he was the chief of police.

"What have we here?" he demanded, swinging about in his chair and eyeing the two severely.

"Prisoners, sir, whom I am instructed to turn over to you," was the orderly's reply. "You are to hold them until you receive further instructions, sir."

"Very good," said the chief. "You may go."

The orderly saluted, turned on his heel and departed.

"You may sit there until I have completed this piece of work," said the chief, motioning the prisoners to chairs behind him.

Hal and Uncle John sat down and the chief turned again to his desk and was soon busy writing.

Hal's eyes roved about the room. An idea struck him like a flash. They sat between the chief of police and the door by which they had entered. What would be more easy than to tip-toe to the door, which stood slightly ajar, and disappear unbeknown to the chief?

With Hal to think was to act. Fearing to lift his voice in a whisper, he at last managed to catch Uncle John's eye. Then he laid a warning finger to his lips and beckoned Uncle John to follow him. Uncle John manifested some surprise, but he signified that he understood.

Carefully Hal got to his feet and Uncle John followed suit. Then Hal, stepping very softly, moved toward the door. Now it was five, now four, now three paces away—and then the boy laid his hand on the knob. Uncle John was right behind him.

The door swung open without so much as a creak, and Hal stepped out. Uncle John followed him. Hal motioned Uncle John to lead the way down the hall, while he remained behind to close the door. The order was obeyed.

Hal took the precaution to close the door tightly and then hurried after Uncle John. "Well—" began Uncle John, just as they stepped from the building, "I guess we—"

Came a sudden roar from behind them—the roar of a human voice.

"The chief!" exclaimed Hal. "Run!"

Uncle John needed no urging and the two went down the steps four and five at a time. Hal led the way and Uncle John followed close at his heels.

Around the corner they darted even as the chief of police appeared in the doorway—too late to see in which direction his erstwhile prisoners had flown. But the two fugitives could hear his voice raised in another roar, as he thundered out a call for his men to give chase.

"Come on, Uncle John!" shouted Hal, and the latter, although he had long since come to believe that his bones had stiffened with age, surprised himself by the manner in which he flew over the ground.

Fortunately, the street at the moment was deserted. Around one, two, then three corners Hal doubled, and then slowed down.

"Guess we are all right for a few minutes," he gasped.

Uncle John stopped and gasped for breath.

"I'm not as young as I used to be, Hal," he said. "Don't forget that. I can't go a hundred yards in eleven seconds any more."

"Well, you didn't miss it much," said Hal, with a chuckle. "But come on, we must get away from here. If we are caught now, the chances are they will stand us up against a wall and have a shot at us."

"In which event," said Uncle John dryly, "I can still do a hundred yards in ten flat."

Side by side the two walked on.

"The question that now arises," said Uncle John, "is how we are going to get away from here?"

"First," said Hal, "we must go back and see if Chester is still where we left him."

"Like looking for a needle in a haystack," said Uncle John. "This is a pretty good-sized town."

"Not at all," replied Hal. "I have a pretty keen sense of

direction; besides, I always make it a point to look at the names of the streets. I can find it in half an hour. Come on."

The lad had not boasted and less than an hour later they stood again in the house where so lately they had been prisoners.

"Well, he's gone," said Hal quietly. "We cannot help him here. The best thing for us to do is to return to Rome and lay the case before the ambassador, who can take the matter up with Ambassador Penfield at Vienna, or through Washington."

"The thing to do, then, is to hunt the railroad station," declared Uncle John. "Do you think you can find it?"

"If I can't, I can ask," replied Hal.

Thirty minutes later saw Hal at the ticket window asking what time the next train left for Rome.

"In an hour," was the reply.

Hal purchased two tickets. Then with Uncle John he strolled about the station.

Suddenly the boy halted in his tracks and grabbed Uncle John by the arm, pulling him into a corner. And it was well that he did so, for a moment later there brushed by the spot where they had stood none other than the chief of police and several other men in uniform.

"He may not be looking for us, but the chances are he is," said Hal.

The chief went straight to the ticket office, where he engaged the agent in conversation.

"No Rome for us now," declared Hal. "Come on."

He led the way out of the station and directly stood in the train shed. The boy heard a cry of "All aboard" and saw that a train was about to pull out.

"Don't know where it is going, but we'll get it!" he cried, and Uncle John followed him in his mad dash. By a hard run they succeeded in climbing into an unoccupied compartment even as the guard would have closed the door.

"Where do you suppose we are bound?" asked Uncle John, as he sat down, panting.

"Don't know," was Hal's reply. "We'll find out directly."

A few minutes later the conductor enlightened them.

"Milan," he said.

CHAPTER XIX

WITH THE ARMY

"Milan!" echoed Hal. "Good night!"

"Oh, well," said Uncle John, with rare optimism for him, "I guess we can double back from there, can't we?"

"I suppose it can be done," agreed Hal. "But we haven't any business wandering all over this country. We want to get to Rome."

"We'll get there, all right," said Uncle John.

"Yes; but if they happen to nab us we are likely not to get there whole," declared Hal.

When the train arrived in Milan, Hal and Uncle John were among the first to alight.

"Well, here we are; now what?" demanded Uncle John.

"You've got me," declared Hal.

They made their way to the street and there they halted suddenly, for a wonderful sight had met their gaze.

Passing along the street were thousands and thousands of soldiers, mounted and afoot, fully equipped for the field. They passed by in a steady stream. For an hour Hal and Uncle John watched the imposing sight and still the long line wended its way along. Hal's heart beat faster as his eyes rested upon this imposing array of fighting strength.

"By Jove! I'd like to go along," he muttered to himself.

And it was to be so, even sooner that he could possibly have hoped. But the suggestion came from an altogether unexpected source.

"Tell you what, Hal," said Uncle John suddenly. "As long as we are here we might as well see a little something. What do you think?"

"Just what do you mean?" asked Hal.

"Well, let's go along to the front with these fellows; that is, if we can make it. We may see something that we will never have another chance to see."

"Suits me," declared Hal. "Let's see if we can get a couple of horses—it's pretty tough walking and we don't know how far we may have to go."

This was easier than could have been expected; and an hour later found them riding slowly along in the direction taken by the Italian troops.

"Don't suppose the authorities here have been apprised of our escape from Milan," said Hal. "I guess we are safe enough."

Hour after hour they rode along, passing regiment after regiment of infantry as it moved toward the front. Uncle

John was greatly impressed by the military carriage and bearing of the troops, but in spite of their impressiveness Hal could not help thinking that they did not have the business-like appearance of the British troops.

Now, in the distance, they made out what they could see was a great camp, stretching out as far as the eye could see on both sides.

"This," said Hal, pointing, "will be the end of our tour of inspection. Beyond those lines they will not let us go."

"We'll go as far as we can," declared Uncle John.

Suddenly from directly ahead came the heavy thunder of a single gun, followed almost immediately by another giant voice. Other big guns began to speak, and soon the roaring of thousands filled the air.

"A battle!" exclaimed Hal.

Other voices now, more faint but sharper of note, took up the fighting—rapid firers and the rifles of the infantry coming into play. From their present position Hal and Uncle John could not tell just where the fighting was in progress, the numbers engaged, or whether the Italians had taken the offensive, or the Austrians, or how the battle was progress-sing. All they could hear was the terrible din and roar. They could see nothing. They were at present far from the battle line.

Still they advanced.

Now they were suddenly in the center of the Italian troops, still stationary, awaiting the word to move forward in sup-port of the second line or the first line as the case might be.

An officer rode up to them.

"What are you doing here?" he demanded.

"Nothing particularly," replied Hal. "I am a British officer and, being in this neighborhood, thought I would look around a bit."

"Your papers?" was the next command.

"Unfortunately, I have none with me," returned the lad.

The officer hesitated.

"I'll tell you," he said finally, "there is a British officer commanding a regiment here. Perhaps he will know you. I shall conduct you to him. He has arrived from France only recently."

"I don't know all the British officers in France," said Hal, "but there is always the possibility I may know this one."

"Follow me," commanded the Italian.

The two did so. To the far left wing their guide led the way, and finally stopped before a tent somewhat larger than the rest.

An orderly came forth.

"Tell the colonel I have a man here who claims to be a British officer," said the Italian.

A moment later there stepped from the tent a long, tall Englishman, attired in British uniform, youngish of face, and at sight of him Hal started forward with a glad cry.

"Major Anderson!" he exclaimed.

The officer gazed at him in surprise, then came forward with extended hand.

"Bless my soul," he exclaimed. "What in the name of all that's wonderful are you doing here? I thought you were dead. And where is Chester?"

"I don't know," answered Hal, answering the last question first.

Upon Colonel Anderson's—he was no longer major—request, Hal plunged into an account of what had transpired since they had last seen the gallant Englishman. Now the Italian officer stepped forward.

"Then they are all right?" he questioned, indicating Hal and Uncle John.

"This one is," replied Anderson, laying a hand on Hal's shoulder. "I don't know the other."

He hastened to introduce the two men.

Anderson turned to the Italian.

"It's all right," he said.

The latter saluted and moved away.

"While you are here," said Anderson, "you will make yourselves at home in my quarters. I am now called to the front."

"Can't we go with you?" asked Hal anxiously.

The colonel hesitated.

"Well, I guess it can be done," he said at length. "You have your horses; wait until I get mine."

A command to his orderly and the horse was soon waiting. The three rode forward and as they went the colonel explained something of the situation and his reason for being with the Italian army.

"I was sent here immediately Italy declared war," he said, "at the request of the Italian government. Of course, they didn't ask for me personally, but they did ask for a British officer who had seen active service. General French selected me, with the rank of colonel. That's why I'm here."

"And this fighting now?" questioned Hal. "Who is on the offensive?"

"The Austrians, at the moment," was the reply. "They have massed thousands of men to the north, and at the far side of the Alps. We have let it be known that we were in insufficient strength here and the Austrians evidently hope, by a quick drive, to gain a foothold on Italian soil. Fortunately, however, our lines were strengthened no later than yesterday and reinforcements still are arriving. The Austrians have delayed too long.

"Now our troops are falling back slowly and in good order. The Austrians, feeling sure of a quick victory, will follow them too far. Then for our coup. First the artillery, then the infantry and cavalry, and let me tell you something, this Italian artillery fire is going to be one of the wonders of the war. Its effect will be terrific. Watch and see."

In the distance now the three made out a squad of a dozen

men advancing toward them, with what appeared to be two prisoners in their midst.

"We'll have a look and see what's up," declared Colonel Anderson.

They rode forward.

As at last they were able to make out the faces of the two apparent prisoners, Hal uttered a loud shout and spurred his horse forward. Uncle John took a second look and did likewise. Colonel Anderson rode rapidly after them.

At the side of the squad, Hal leaped quickly from his horse, and plunging directly into the squad, threw his arms about one of the prisoners.

"Chester!" he cried.

And Chester it was.

The latter returned his friend's embrace with gusto, and then freeing himself, fell into the bear hug of Uncle John.

The latter was sniffling with joy; but at last released, Chester caught sight of Colonel Anderson.

Again there was an affectionate greeting and then Hal heard a voice in his ear.

"And haven't you anything to say to me, young man?"

Hal whirled about and caught sight of the smiling face of Anthony Stubbs, war correspondent of the New York *Gazette*.

"Stubbs!" he cried, and his delight was so evident that the little man flushed with pleasure.

Introductions followed all around now and then Colonel Anderson addressed the officer in charge of the squad.

"Are these men prisoners?" he asked.

"No, sir," was the reply, "but General Ferrari instructed me to have them taken to a place of safety."

"Then you can turn them over to me without question?"

"Yes, sir."

"Good! Then I shall relieve you of further responsibility."

The Italian saluted, ordered his men to "'Bout face" and marched off toward the front.

CHAPTER XX

THE ADVANCE

The shrill, clear voice of a single bugle broke the stillness of the early morning. There was a second of intense silence, and the call came again. A second took it up, and a third, and many more, each less distinct than the first, for they were farther away.

Hal, Chester, Uncle John and Anthony Stubbs, three of them accustomed as they were to the life of the military camps, were upon their feet almost before the sound of the first bugle had died away, and strained their ears to catch a repetition.

They had spent the night in a large tent assigned them by Colonel Anderson, not far from his own quarters, and had retired completely exhausted as the result of the strenuous time they had gone through. But they were all perfectly wide awake now and rushed from their tent with the sound of the second call.

"A call to arms!" exclaimed Hal.

"Probably means an advance," said Chester quietly.

"I guess you are right," returned his chum. "And here we are, nothing but spectators at the best."

"And that's where you are lucky," chimed in Stubbs. "Now take me, I've got to get out among all this fighting and maybe I'll be killed. But I've got to do it. You fellows can stay here where it is perfectly safe."

"Well, I'd much rather be in your place, then," said Chester.

"Same here," declared Hal.

The Italian camp had sprung to life as if by magic. Half-clothed sleepers poured from the tents and formed into ranks in the darkness. Officers ran hither and thither shouting hoarse orders. For a moment confusion reigned, but this gave place almost immediately to perfect order. The discipline of the Italian troops was remarkable. In almost less time than it takes to tell it, the whole Italian army of the North, stretching out as it did for mile after mile and mile after mile, was under arms, eagerly awaiting the word that would send it against the strongly entrenched Austrian columns ahead.

Less than a hundred rods away Hal made out the form of Colonel Anderson, as he now stood at the head of his men; gazing steadily ahead except when he turned to give an order to one of his subordinates. Far back, just distinguishable in the now half light, could be seen the dense masses of cavalry, unmounted as yet, but ready to leap to the saddle and dash forward at command.

A gun boomed, shattering the almost oppressive stillness. Another followed suit. More took up the work and the air was filled with their thundering. It became apparent to Hal and Chester, to whom this was nothing new, that the infantry would make the first advance, under the support of the artillery.

"A good-sized job, if you ask me," declared the latter.

"Rather," replied Hal dryly. "Hey," breaking off suddenly, "where are you going?"

"To the front," replied Stubbs, to whom the lad had addressed his remark, pausing for a moment and glancing back over his shoulder. "Got to get a little news, you know."

"You'd better look out or you are likely to get a little bullet," remarked Uncle John.

"Well, I'll have to take a chance," replied the little man.

With a wave of his hand he disappeared in the darkness.

"Forward!" came a clear voice from their rear.

Came the heavy tramp, tramp of marching feet, as the First Infantry moved forward. Steadily they marched ahead, silently and with an air of determination. They made an imposing appearance in the dim light of early morning.

"A gallant body of men," muttered Hal. "They'll give a good account of themselves."

Came a word of command from Colonel Anderson—the boys recognized his voice—and more troops moved forward. As far as the eye could see dense masses of men were marching rapidly toward the front. It became apparent that this was to be no mere skirmish—no mere feeling-out process. It was to be a battle, and as both lads realized, it might well last for days.

"We may as well go forward a bit," said Hal.

Accordingly the three started out. Half an hour later they were suddenly surrounded by a body of infantry, and, in some unaccountable manner, were separated from Uncle John. In vain they looked, called and whistled for him. He had disappeared.

"Well, I guess he will be able to find the way back," said Chester. "We'd better see if we can find him."

They retraced their steps. For an hour and more they waited, but Uncle John failed to put in an appearance. And all the time, from ahead, came the dull roar of battle.

"Well, what shall we do?" asked Chester at length.

Hal shrugged his shoulders.

"Guess your peaceful Uncle John has gone on to the front," he said. "We may as well do the same. He'll turn up sooner or later."

Chester was struck with a sudden idea.

"By Jove!" he exclaimed.

"What's the matter now?" demanded Hal, eyeing his chum in some surprise.

"I was just thinking," said Chester. "Say, let's see if we can't find a couple of spare uniforms around here."

"H-m-m," muttered Hal, who knew what Chester meant. "Maybe we shouldn't do anything like that."

"Maybe we shouldn't," agreed Chester, "but there is no one here to tell us not to. Come on."

Hal followed him.

They looked into several tents, but their search met with no success, but in the sixth tent they were more fortunate. Chester, rummaging around in a corner, produced a lieutenant's uniform.

"Looks like it might fit," he said. "I'll try it on."

He did.

"Fits well enough," he said.

"All right," said Hal. "But where is mine?"

"Oh, we'll find you one, all right," said Chester.

And, after half an hour's further search, they did—a second lieutenant's uniform. Hal donned it hurriedly.

"Might as well hunt up our horses," he said.

"Ours?" queried Chester.

"Well, mine and Uncle John's, or anybody else's, for that matter. It's a long walk to the front."

They were fortunate enough to find two mounts without much trouble, and, leaping to the saddles, they rode forward.

"Got a gun?" asked Chester.

"No," replied Hal. "Have you?"

"No such luck. Maybe we can find one further on."

This hope was realized.

As they rode forward the sights of battle became evident. Here and there were fallen men, some dead and some dying, struck down by the long-range artillery of the Austrians. Red Cross nurses and physicians were busy attending to the wounded.

Hal leaped to the ground, and from the fingers of a dead officer took a revolver. A second he removed from his holster. Then he unstrapped the officer's sword belt and put it on himself.

"Well, I'm fixed," he said, leaning down and producing the unfortunate officer's supply of ammunition.

"My turn next," said Chester.

Half a mile further along he relieved a second fallen officer of his sword, revolvers and ammunition.

"Now," said he, "we are ready to go into battle?"

"We're ready," agreed Hal, "but we have no business there."

"Well, we won't do any fighting unless we have to," said Chester, "but we'll go as far to the front as we can."

They rode forward more rapidly.

Meanwhile, the Italians pressed forward to the attack. With the first shell hurled within their lines by the enemy's artillery, the Austrians came to life. Weak spots in the long battle line were strengthened, reinforcements were hurried forward all along the entire front. The Austrian artillery opened fire and for an hour the long-range artillery duel continued.

But now the Austrian officers grew greatly excited. From the shelter of the distant Italian trenches rose a long line of men. Coolly they formed under the Austrian fire, and stood awaiting the signal to advance. And a moment later it came.

On came the Italians in spite of the withering fire of the Austrian infantry and the still more deadly execution of the great guns, which mowed them down by the hundreds.

But as fast as these gaps appeared, they were filled by others, and the Italians continued to forge ahead.

An Austrian bugle spoke sharply, and there sallied forth from the Austrian entrenchments masses of infantry at the double, closely followed by cavalry.

Evidently the Austrian commander had determined not to put his entire dependence upon his artillery.

The Italians sprang forward to meet the foe. They rushed as though hurled from a catapult.

The solid lines of infantry met with a shock. Rifles flashed and revolvers spoke sharply. Steel flashed in the air and hand grenades added their deadly execution to the terrible work.

And now the Italian infantry parted suddenly in the center and from behind at a furious pace came squadron upon squadron of cavalry, possibly, all told, five thousand men.

With impetuous bravery they dashed forward, throwing themselves upon the bayonets of the Austrian infantry, which had braced to receive the shock. But the enemy could not withstand this desperate charge. They faltered, hesitated, broke and fled. In vain their officers sought to bring order out of chaos. It was beyond their effort.

Straight in among the broken infantry plunged the Italian cavalry. Sabers whirled in the air and descended with terrible effect. Horses trampled fallen men, and bit at those who stood in their way, stamping and striking at others with their feet.

Realizing that his infantry was completely demoralized, the Austrian commander gave the word to send his own cavalry into the fray.

With a shout the horsemen charged. The Italians drew up their horses sharply and braced themselves to meet this new attack.

Chester and Hal, who came within view of this deadly work at this moment, stood spellbound.

Then Chester spoke.

"Now," he said, "you will see what I call real fighting. Look!"

The two bodies of horsemen met with a crash.

CHAPTER XXI

THE BOYS GO INTO BATTLE

Sitting their horses quietly, their lives endangered every moment by shot and shell that dropped around them and whistled by their heads, Hal and Chester watched keenly the hand-to-hand struggle that ensued.

The two bodies of horsemen met with a crash less than a quarter of a mile from where the two lads had taken their places. With swords and sabers flashing aloft, the Austrians had charged with a wild yell. The Italian cavalry, stationary and braced for the shock, received their foes silently.

Hal and Chester could see that the opposing bodies of horse were about evenly matched; and they realized that skill, horsemanship and fighting prowess would play important parts in the encounter.

The very fierceness of the Austrian charge swept away the front rank of the Italian cavalry; and, over the fallen bodies of men and horses the foe pressed on, taking no count of their own dead and injured that reeled and fell from the saddles. The horses themselves became imbued with the spirit of battle, and bit and struck at each other as their riders fought with sword, saber and pistol.

It was a terrible sight, and the lads shuddered unconsciously. It was more frightful to the spectator than it was to the struggling men themselves, who, in the heat of battle, took no thought of the dead and the dying and pressed forward bent only upon protecting themselves while they sought the lives of their foes.

For an hour the fierce hand-to-hand struggle raged, with advantage apparently first to one side and then to the other. In other sections of the field, at least where Hal and Chester could see, operations had ceased for the moment, each commander evidently loath to hurl forward additional troops until the cavalry action had been decided. However, the troops were engaged in other quarters of the field. Upon the right the Italians had made no impression on the Austrian, but the Italian left wing had had better success. The first line of trenches of the enemy had fallen to the attacking forces after a fierce bayonet charge by the infantry, and the left wing had now taken shelter in the trenches and was preparing to beat off a counter attack which the Austrian commander even now was about to make.

And in the center the cavalry still fought sullenly and fiercely.

Suddenly Hal uttered an exclamation of dismay.

From a quarter of a mile to the left of the struggling cavalry, a second body of Austrian horsemen appeared. These men had been ordered to make a detour and fall upon the Italian horse from the left. They now charged with a shout.

Apparently this had taken the Italian commander by surprise, for no additional Italian troops were for the moment hurled forward to the support of the cavalry. Beset by this new foe, the Italians were forced back slowly, fighting every minute, however, and contesting every foot of ground as they retreated.

Hal and Chester now realized for the first time that they were directly in the line of retreat.

"We'd better move, Hal," said Chester, "or we shall have to fight whether we want to or not."

Hal signified his assent with a nod of his head, and they turned their horses' heads to ride out of harm's way.

But they had delayed too long.

From behind them came a loud, terrible, blood-curdling shout, and gazing quickly about, the lads saw that they were directly in the road of large cavalry reinforcements that were being rushed forward to the support of the hard-pressed men in front.

"Quick, Chester!" cried Hal, and put spurs to his horse.

But it was too late.

The Italian cavalry was upon them, and rather than be thrown down and trampled, the lads were forced to turn their horses in with the troop; and thus they were carried along like a whirlwind in the very front rank of the charge, and Hal, glancing to his left, felt a sudden sense of satisfaction as he saw that the man who led this desperate charge was none other than Colonel Harry Anderson, his old companion in arms, the man by whose side both he and Chester had faced death more than once.

Hal's hand dropped to his belt, and his revolver came forth in his left hand. The reins he allowed to fall loose upon his horse's neck, while with his right hand he drew his sword. Chester, with the light of battle in his eyes, was already prepared.

The horses of the two boys darted forward with the rest of the troop, their ears standing straight up, their manes bristling, their nostrils extended.

Now the troop came close upon the cavalry already engaged; and these men, despite their seeming confusion, parted as though by a prearranged plan, and the reinforcements passed through, and fell upon the enemy with an impact that was not to be denied. Behind, the first troop reformed and now came forward in support.

And once more Hal and Chester found themselves in the midst of battle.

Just before the impact, and as Colonel Anderson brandished his sword aloft and urged his men on with a shouted command, Hal discharged his revolver at a tall Austrian who had taken deliberate aim at Colonel Anderson. The man threw up his hands and with a wild yell toppled beneath the feet of the plunging horses, there to be trampled to death if Hal's bullet had not been enough.

One volley was poured into the Austrians at a command from Colonel Anderson, and then the Italians were upon the foe with drawn sabers. A single volley from the Austrians proved ineffective; Hal and Chester and the commander of the troop were unscathed and the Austrians had no time for another.

Chester parried a blow aimed at him by an Austrian cavalryman, and raising his pistol quickly, toppled him from his horse with a bullet. A second ploughed its way through the chest of another trooper and with his sword the lad caught a blow that at that moment would have descended upon Hal's head.

And so the fighting went, cut, thrust, parry and strike, with an occasional revolver shot in between; and Hal, Chester, and Colonel Anderson, in some miraculous manner, escaping injury.

The Austrians fought bravely, giving blow for blow, and in the center succeeded in breaking through. It was but a mere handful of men who succeeded in this venture, however, and they were immediately cut off from their friends. A demand to surrender went unheeded; and a moment later they had gone down.

A bugle sounded in the Austrian rear. The enemy drew off. It was first blood to the Italians and the troops raised a loud cheer as they dashed forward in pursuit of the foe, who now turned their horses about sharply and fled.

For a hundred yards the Italians pursued, doing great execution with their heavy cavalry swords; and then Colonel Anderson called a halt, for he feared he might be rushing into a trap.

When two hundred yards separated the opposing forces, the Austrian artillery suddenly broke loose again. A shell struck squarely in the center of the Italian horsemen, doing frightful execution. Colonel Anderson hurriedly gave the order to fall back.

The colonel turned to Hal and Chester.

"What are you two doing here?" he demanded. "I thought you told me your fighting days were over?"

"We thought so, too," replied Hal, with a smile, "but you fellows swooped down on us so suddenly that we didn't have a chance to get out of the way."

"And it seemed pretty good," said Chester, "just like old times."

"You both gave good accounts of yourselves," declared the colonel. "I'll have a word to say about you in my report."

"No use of—" began Chester and broke off with an ejaculation: "Hello!"

"What's up?" demanded Anderson.

For answer, Chester pointed to the left and slightly ahead. There, overlooked in some way, a small body of Italian troops was engaged silently with a larger number of Austrians and the Italians were getting the worst of the encounter.

Colonel Anderson made his decision in a moment, and in spite of the Austrian artillery shells that were flying overhead and dropping on all sides, the cavalry rushed to the aid of their countrymen.

But the Austrians didn't wait to receive this new attack. They turned and took to their heels; and as they hastened away, Hal caught the sound of a voice coming from their midst:

"Hal! Chester!" it came. "Help!"

"By George! it's Uncle John!" exclaimed Chester, and urged his horse forward faster than before.

"Uncle John—and a prisoner," ejaculated Hal, and also

spurred forward.

But a heavy hand was laid on the bridle of each.

"Here! what's the matter with you fellows?" demanded Colonel Anderson's gruff voice. "Want to get yourselves killed?"

"But we've got to get Uncle John out of this mess," declared Chester.

"You won't get him out by getting yourselves killed," was the reply. "He's safe enough now. He's a prisoner and they won't hurt him."

"But they'll keep him prisoner," was Chester's exclamation.

"Well, what of it?" demanded the colonel.

"Well, I don't know," said Chester slowly.

"I'll speak to the general," said Colonel Anderson. "Perhaps he will see his way clear to making representations for his release."

"Do you think he will?" asked Hal eagerly.

"To tell you the truth, I don't, but I'll speak to him, anyhow."

With this the lads were forced to be content, for they realized that Colonel Anderson would not permit them to go forward by themselves; besides, they recognized the folly of such an act.

The battle was over for the moment. The Italian left wing retained the ground won despite several counter assaults and the right wing had also been pushed forward after vigorous fighting. The Italians held their dearly gained victory in the center.

"Come with me," said Colonel Anderson to Hal and Chester. "We'll have a talk with the general."

The two lads followed him.

CHAPTER XXII

OFF ON A MISSION

"I regret to say that what you ask is impossible."

The speaker was General Ferrari, commander of the Italian army of the North—the army that later was to attempt an invasion of Austrian territory by way of the Alps.

Colonel Anderson had just put before the general the question of trying to gain the freedom of Uncle John. The general turned to Hal and Chester.

"I am not unmindful of the great help you rendered Italy in Rome," he said; "but, at the same time, I cannot grant your present request. I am sorry."

"Why, that's all right, sir," said Chester quietly. "The idea was Colonel Anderson's, and if it cannot be done, that settles it, of course. Uncle John will have to take his chances, the same as the rest of us."

"I am glad you are so sensible about it," replied the general. "Now," turning to Colonel Anderson, "I have a matter to discuss with you."

Hal and Chester took their departure, telling Colonel Anderson they would await him without. Half an hour later the colonel joined them.

"It's too bad you fellows are not in the fighting business any more," he said.

"Why?" demanded both lads in one voice.

"Because I am now confronted with a piece of work in which I should be glad to have your aid."

"What kind of work?" asked Chester.

"Oh, just a little mission that would take us into the Austrian lines. General Ferrari wants a little information, and he has selected me to go after it. I've got to have a couple of companions."

"By Jove, Chester! Here's a chance for us," declared Hal. "We'll go along, and who knows, perhaps we may have a chance to help Uncle John, too."

"Good!" agreed Chester. "What do you say, colonel?"

"I am afraid the general would not hear of it," replied the colonel, with a slight smile. "For my part, if you are willing I should be glad to have you with me. I know you are to be depended upon and I have great confidence in your resourcefulness."

"Let's go and see the general," said Chester.

Colonel Anderson offered no protest to this and a few moments later Chester put his request to General Ferrari.

"H-m-m," said the general, musing for a while. Then he gave his decision. "All right," he said; "but first, I want to impress one thing upon you. Your work of trying to release your Uncle John, as you call him, must be a secondary matter. The mission you are undertaking will permit of no delay. Do you agree to that?"

"Yes, sir," replied both lads, without an instant's hesitation.

"You say you hold commissions in the Belgian army?" asked the general.

"Yes, and I can vouch for the fact that they were both attached to the staff of General Sir John French," put in Colonel Anderson.

"Very well, then," returned the general. "You may go, and my only instructions are that the work be done with the greatest possible haste."

"It shall be done, sir," declared the colonel. "Come, boys."

The three saluted and made their way from the general's quarters.

In Colonel Anderson's tent they talked over their plans.

"Just what is it we are supposed to find out?" asked Hal.

"First, the enemy's strength at this point," replied the colonel. "The lay of the land, the strength of the enemy's position, how his army is laid out, and, lastly, the feasibility of a quick dash over the Alps."

"Not such a little job, after all," commented Hal dryly.

"And," said Chester, "just how do you figure we are going to get within the Austrian lines?"

"That's the problem," said the colonel. "We'll have to figure that out. One thing, we've got to get there, and at least one of us has got to get back again. Luckily, I speak German fluently. I don't believe Austrian will be necessary."

"Not much difference, is there?" asked Hal.

"Some. But German will do us."

"Well," said Chester, "one thing is certain; we shall have to discard our uniforms."

"In which event," said Hal, "we shall be shot if captured."

"That can't be helped," said the colonel. "We'll have to don civilian garb."

"But how to get across?"

"Say, look here, I've got a plan," said Chester.

"Let's have it," said Hal.

"Listen, then. We'll put on civilian clothes. We'll tell the Italian officer in command of the farthest outpost what we are about to do. We'll get horses and we'll have a squadron of Italian cavalry chase us, shooting—but over our heads. That will attract the enemy, and they'll come forward to help us. Then we'll get there."

"But what reason will we give for wanting to get into the Austrian lines?" asked Hal.

Clair W. Hayes

"I'm coming to that. Before we start, we'll draw up a couple of maps of supposed Italian positions—which, of course, will be directly the opposite of how things are here; we'll take down false figures of the Italian strength and other such things. We'll tell the Austrian commander, when we are taken before him, that we are German secret agents, and we'll get away with it. Fortunately, I think we know the phrase that will get us by."

"What do you mean?" asked Hal.

"Why, the one you used on Robard in Rome," said Chester. "'From the Wilhelmstrasse.'"

"By Jove! I believe you are right," declared Hal.

"I am certain of it," replied Chester. "So, you see, we will overcome suspicion, and will have freedom of the Austrian camp—practically. Now, what do you think of the plan?"

"Well, it has its advantages," replied Colonel Anderson, "and if we are careful and cautious, it may work. In lieu of a better, I guess we may as well act upon it. Now, who is going to draw these maps? A map I would draw wouldn't look like much."

"I guess that is up to me," said Chester. "I am rather handy with a pencil."

He set to work and an hour later produced the result of his labors.

"Fine," said the colonel, after gazing at the maps. "And you have laid them out, names and all. If the Austrians were to advance with the belief that these were authentic, we'd eat 'em alive."

"I hope they do it," said Chester. "Now it's up to you to get the other figures."

"We've prepared those," said the colonel, and produced the result of an hour's work.

"Now we'll have to hide them, so it will look right," said Chester.

"Right; but first crumple them up and rub a little dirt on 'em," said Hal.

This was done.

Then the three went in search of the necessary clothing. This they obtained without much difficulty.

"Now, about the starting time?" said Chester.

"My idea," said Hal, "is that we go to the front at once, but that we do not start toward the enemy's lines until just after the break of day."

"Why?" asked Colonel Anderson.

"For several reasons, but one will suffice. If we go at night the whole thing is likely to go wrong, and they'll shoot us without taking any chances. They won't see our apparently serious predicament in the darkness."

"You are right, as usual," replied the colonel.

"Now about weapons," said Chester. "We ought to carry a couple of guns apiece."

"And a good supply of ammunition," agreed Hal.

"We've got the guns, but not the ammunition," said Chester.

"I'll rustle that up for you in a few minutes," said the colonel.

He was as good as his word.

An hour later they set out for the front, still in uniform, for they did not wish to don their civilian attire until it became necessary, for fear they would arouse suspicion in the breast of the Italian officer in command and necessitate a loss of time.

The Italian colonel in command of the outpost at the extreme northern front listened to their plan and pronounced it a good one.

"I'll have you chased good and properly," he said, with a grin.

"Guess we had better turn in," said Colonel Anderson. "We'll leave it to you to have us called half an hour before daybreak," he said to the officer.

"I'll have you up if I have to pull you out by the heels myself," was the reply.

The three friends turned in in the officer's own tent and soon were fast asleep, their desperate mission of the morrow weighing not at all upon their minds. They were too seasoned veterans for that.

Half an hour before daybreak they were aroused. All were perfectly wide awake in a moment and donned their civilian clothes. Then they left the tent and joined the Italian officer, where he awaited their coming and explained to the officer of a squadron of cavalry what was expected of him.

The latter nodded his understanding of the order and repeated it to his men.

It was cool in the early morning air, close to the mountains as they were, and the boys shivered a bit. Both were anxious for the time for action.

A faint tinge of gray streaked the eastern sky; and gradually it grew brighter.

"Well, guess we may as well be on our way," said the colonel. "Have you got our horses?"

The animals were led up at a command from the Italian officer. The three swung themselves to the saddles.

"Ready?" queried the colonel, gazing carefully around.

"All ready," came the reply.

"Good! Here we go then," and the colonel set off at a gallop, his revolver in his hand. Hal and Chester spurred after him.

CHAPTER XXIII

WITHIN THE ENEMY'S LINES

Revolvers clasped tightly in both hands, the reins hanging loose on their horses' necks, while they guided the animals by the pressure of the knees, the friends dashed forward toward the Austrian lines, probably three miles ahead.

When they had gone some two hundred yards, there came behind them, with loud shouts, a squadron of Italian cavalry, firing as they urged their mounts on.

A hundred yards farther on the three saw signs of excitement in the Austrian ranks, now visible in the distance. A moment and a troop sallied forth to protect the flight of the apparent fugitives, and to drive back the Italians.

Hal, thinking to help the illusion along, pulled his horse up sharply, and as the animal staggered and lost his stride, the lad tumbled off. He was up in a moment, however, and raising his revolver, emptied it at the Italian horsemen bearing down on him. He was careful to aim high, however.

Chester and Colonel Anderson checked their mounts and the former leaped to the ground and helped Hal back to his saddle. Then, with a last volley in the direction of the

Italians, they urged their horses on again.

Meanwhile they could hear the whine of the Italian bullets above their head, some so close that Chester feared for a moment the Italian cavalrymen had misunderstood their orders. But none touched them.

Straight toward the onrushing Austrians they spurred their horses; and the Austrians parted to let them through. At this juncture the Italians gave up the chase and retired; and the Austrians did not pursue them.

"Pretty narrow escape you fellows had," said the Austrian officer, speaking in German.

"Rather," replied Hal dryly. "When my horse stumbled back there, I was afraid it was all over."

"I thought so myself," returned the Austrian. "But what is the matter? Who are you?"

Hal gazed about sharply, and then leaning close to the Austrian, whispered:

"From the Wilhelmstrasse."

The Austrian never moved a muscle, but whispered back again:

"Good! Then you desire to see General Brentz?"

"At once, if you please," replied Hal.

The Austrian nodded.

Back within his own lines the officer volunteered to conduct the three to the general himself.

"It will avoid delay," he explained.

The three friends followed him.

Before the quarters of the Austrian commander, the officer whispered to the orderly stationed at the entrance. The latter saluted and disappeared. He came out a moment later and motioned for all to enter.

A large man, both tall and stout, was General Brentz, and he eyed the three with a close gaze. All gave the stiff German military salute.

"You come from—" said the general, and paused.

"The Wilhelmstrasse," said Colonel Anderson, leaning slightly forward.

"And how did you get here?"

"Well, not without some trouble," replied the colonel. "And we almost failed. But, fortunately, we remembered that the Wilhelmstrasse never fails, and with the aid of your cavalry, sir, we escaped. This officer," pointing to the man who had conducted them there, "can perhaps tell you better than I. I was too busy with my horse."

The officer, at the general's command, gave an account of the chase.

"Very well," said the general, when he had concluded. He turned again to Colonel Anderson. "I take it you have valuable information for me, then?"

"Yes, sir, but for you only," replied the colonel, nodding toward the other officer.

General Brentz took the hint. He motioned the subordinate to withdraw.

Colonel Anderson leaned down and unloosened his boot. He took it off, and drawing a knife from his pocket, slit the sole. Then he withdrew several sheets of dirty, crumpled paper, which he extended to General Brentz. The latter took them eagerly, and turned quickly to his desk.

For almost an hour he poured over the papers and at last a slow smile spread itself over his face. He turned to the others.

"This," he said, "will prove the very link for which I have been wishing. I may need more information from you, sirs."

The three friends were afraid to look at each other for fear they would betray themselves, so all stood silent.

"I take it you know something of my position here," said General Brentz to Colonel Anderson.

"Very little, sir," was the reply.

"I'll show you," said the general. "Draw up chairs, gentlemen; you may be able to help me."

The three did as requested and then the Austrian commander spread a big map on the desk.

"Here," he said, "are the positions of my troops. Now, having in mind the lay of the enemy forces, can you not see that a feint on the enemy left wing, followed by an attack in force

Clair W. Hayes

on the center, is the key to the whole situation?"

Colonel Anderson nodded his head slowly. In the meantime he was looking carefully at the map before him, impressing it upon his memory, as were Hal and Chester also.

The colonel put a finger on the map.

"Then the bulk of your men are massed here?" he asked, indicating the center.

"No, that's the beauty of it," was the reply. "My strength is on my left wing. But an attack in force in the center, after a feint with my right, will call such Italian troops to the center that a second assault in force on our left will be almost certain of success."

"I see," said the colonel slowly. "You are right, sir. And what is the strength, approximately, of your left wing?"

"One hundred and fifty thousand men. Fifty to seventy-five thousand in the center and somewhat under fifty thousand in the right wing."

"Enough to make a show of force at any given point," commented the colonel.

"Exactly; and with these maps and plans you have brought me, there can be no reason for failure."

"Have you ever considered, general," said Hal, "that a raid by the enemy in force of say fifty thousand men, through your right wing, would give them a commanding position in the mountains, a position from which they could not be dislodged without a deal of trouble?"

"It has been one of my worries," was the quiet reply. "But, because of the strategic position of the ground, I cannot afford to weaken my left wing or my center to strengthen it. But if this new plan of mine goes through, it will obviate all danger of such an attack."

"And how long would it take you to prepare for such an attack?" asked Chester.

"I would not attempt it under three days," was the reply. "Besides, feeling sure of success as I do, I will wait for another reason. The Emperor of Germany will be here within the next day or two and I would have him see my troops in action. I trust you will stay here until he arrives. I shall take pleasure in commending you to his Majesty."

"We shall be glad to accept your hospitality until that time," said the colonel, "if you can provide us with suitable quarters."

"It shall be done," said the general and clapped his hands.

An orderly entered and to him the general gave the necessary instructions. As the three would have followed the orderly out, the general stayed them.

"One moment," he said. "I had forgotten you are not in uniform and would be annoyed without a paper giving you the freedom of our lines."

He turned and scribbled for a few moments, and gave each a paper.

"Make yourselves entirely at home," he said. "I shall always be ready to give you an interview providing the press of other work does not interfere."

Clair W. Hayes

Again the three gave the stiff German military salute and the general rose to his feet as he returned it.

Then the three friends followed the orderly from the tent.

An hour later found them established in large and pretentious quarters—a handsomely appointed tent not far from the first-line troops, but still far enough back to be safe from the Italian artillery shells that ever and anon came hurtling across the open.

"Well," said Chester, in a low voice, "we were fortunate."

"We were, indeed," returned the colonel. "I can't imagine yet what possessed the general to let us have a look at that map."

"Nor I," said Hal.

"Well, I've got a picture of it in my mind that will keep for a week," said Chester. "I don't need to draw it."

"And it would be well not to," declared the colonel. "For if anything should happen and you had such a map, you would be shot without a moment's notice."

"There is one thing sure," said Hal. "We'll have to get out of here before the Kaiser arrives. He'll naturally want to have a look at his secret agents and then it would be good night."

"Rather," replied Chester dryly. "Besides, it seems to me that we know enough right now."

"Well, we'll look about another day, anyhow," said the colonel. "We may be able to gather a few more details."

"It won't hurt anything," said Hal. "That's sure."

"Then we'll make our dash for the Italian lines to-morrow night," said Chester.

"Agreed," said Colonel Anderson and Hal.

There was a call from without and a moment later a pleasant, dapper little officer stuck his head in the tent.

"General Brentz has told me to put myself at your service," he said. "Perhaps you would like me to conduct you through the camp?"

The three friends were glad of this chance and followed him.

Clair W. Hayes

CHAPTER XXIV

UNCLE JOHN "BUTTS IN"

"Well," said Chester to the young Austrian officer, as they were returning to their quarters an hour later, "you hold a remarkably strong position here. And still, if you are forced to fall back, then what?"

The Austrian smiled.

"We have considered all possibilities," he replied. "Back there," sweeping his arm about in a comprehensive gesture, "lies Gorizia, the key to Trieste, which naturally is the Italian goal in this section. Gorizia is exceptionally well fortified, as you well know. We could defend ourselves there indefinitely in the face of overwhelming numbers."

"But," interrupted Hal, "it is not necessary to capture Gorizia to take Trieste?"

"No," said the Austrian with a smile, "but it is necessary to take Gorizia to hold Trieste. The mountains that overhang the city are fortified with our great guns, which could rain shells upon the city without danger of a successful reply. The Italians know this, which is the reason they have not struck at Trieste before. The same goes for Trent, the other point coveted by the enemy."

The party had stopped during this discussion, but now moved on again. In this part of the camp the tents were laid out in little streets and avenues, and down these they walked slowly.

And suddenly the three friends were treated to a disagreeable shock.

Closely followed by a guard, Uncle John suddenly stepped from a tent and stood directly in their path. He seemed stricken dumb with amazement for a moment and then hurried up to them with a glad cry.

"Chester! Hal!" he exclaimed in English.

For a moment the two lads were dumbfounded. Then, realizing their perilous situation, Hal pushed Uncle John away and frowned at him. He whirled upon the Austrian officer.

"What is the meaning of this?" he demanded sternly. "I did not know you had lunatics here."

Now Uncle John knew something of German himself, and he caught this remark. He glared angrily at Hal and then spoke to Chester.

"What's the meaning of this, Chester?" he asked.

Chester did not reply, pretending that he did not understand English. Uncle John grew more angry.

"You young scalawags," he shouted, "what are you trying to do? Have some fun with me? I want to tell you this is no place nor time for fun. I want to get out of here."

Hal and Chester each was afraid to give Uncle John a signal for fear it might be seen and Colonel Anderson made no move to interfere. The Austrian officer turned a suspicious gaze upon the three friends.

"Do you know this man?" he asked.

Hal shook his head.

"He evidently has mistaken us for some one else," he said. "Do you understand what he says? It sounds like it was English he spoke."

"So it is," replied the Austrian. "He called you Hal and Chester and also scalawags, whatever that means."

Chester shrugged his shoulders.

"I don't know him," he said.

"Nor I," said Hal.

"I've never seen him before, to my knowledge," declared Colonel Anderson.

The Austrian officer glared down at Uncle John.

"What's the meaning of this?" he demanded in broken English. "Why do you accost these gentlemen?"

"Why?" exclaimed Uncle John, dancing up and down in his rage, "why? Because one of them is my nephew. What does he want to deny he knows me for?"

"He says one of you is his nephew," said the Austrian turning to the others.

"Well, he's wrong," declared Chester. "I'm sure none of us ever saw him before. Let us go."

The Austrian signified his readiness and they moved off; and as they went along Uncle John, glaring after them, shook a finger violently, and shouted time after time:

"You young rascals. You'll be sorry for this."

He was still raging when the others disappeared from sight among the tents.

"I wonder why?" he asked himself repeatedly, when he was back in his prison tent. And then suddenly it dawned upon him. "What a fool I was," he muttered. "Of course they are here to get me out of this and I came almost spoiling the whole thing, if I have not done so. I ought to be licked."

Meanwhile, the three friends followed the Austrian officer back to their quarters, where he left them.

"By Jove! that was a pretty close shave," remarked Hal, after the officer had taken his leave.

"Rather," replied Chester dryly. "You would think a man of Uncle John's age would have more sense. I'll tell him about it good and strong when I see him again."

"But great Scott! wasn't he mad," said Hal with a laugh. "Did you see how he glared at us? Wonder what he thinks of us, anyhow?"

"Maybe he thinks he has made a mistake," put in the colonel.

"No, he doesn't," declared Chester. "He knows us when he sees us, all right, and I'll bet he is doing some tall thinking about now."

"Well," said the colonel, "we have done about enough for to-day. I vote we accept the officer's invitation to have dinner with him."

"Same here," agreed the others.

The evening and night passed quickly, as did another day, and with the coming of darkness on the second day, the friends began to think of a method of making their way back to their own lines.

"We'll have to make an effort to take Uncle John with us," said Chester.

"Sure," agreed Hal and the colonel, and the latter added: "I guess we will manage it some way. Now, as to the matter of getting by the outposts."

"I can't see as there will be any difficulty about that," said Chester. "Fortunately we are known to most of the officers around here by sight. They will think nothing strange of the fact that we are making a tour of the outposts. Then, if we can manage to catch a sentinel off guard, we can nab him and run."

"Sounds all right," remarked Hal. "We'll try it. But first we must get Uncle John."

"Of course," said the colonel. "We'll get him, all right. In an hour, then, we shall move."

The hour passed slowly, and it seemed to all that the time for action would never come. But at last Colonel Anderson, after a glance at his watch, rose to his feet.

"Let's go," he said briefly.

The others followed him from the tent and he led the way quickly to where Uncle John was confined. In the distance they saw that a sentinel stood on guard and that to enter by that way would arouse suspicion.

"You fellows engage the guard in conversation," said Chester, "and keep talking to him until I rejoin you."

The others asked no questions, but signified that they understood. Chester let them walk on ahead of him, and then made his way to the rear of the row of tents.

He produced a knife when he stood behind Uncle John's tent and slit the canvas silently. Inside Uncle John was reading by candle light. Chester whistled softly, the old whistle of his boyhood days at home, which he felt sure Uncle John would recognize.

Nor was he wrong. Uncle John looked around quickly and beheld Chester's face peering into the tent. Chester laid a finger to his lips and Uncle John nodded. Then Chester beckoned Uncle John to come toward him and the latter did so. Chester enlarged the opening in the tent with his knife and Uncle John stepped into the open.

"Follow me," whispered the lad.

Uncle John asked no questions, but obeyed. Two hundred yards from the tent, Chester halted.

"Now you stay right here till I come back," he said.

He hastened away to join his friends, who were still talking to Uncle John's guard.

Clair W. Hayes

He joined in the conversation for a moment and then announced that they might as well turn in. They told the guard good night and walked back to where Chester had left Uncle John. The latter greeted them with silent joy; he realized that to make a sound might betray them, and he was tired of standing there by himself.

Colonel Anderson motioned to the others to follow and led the way forward.

Swiftly and silently the four shadowy forms made their way along in the shelter of the innumerable tents; and finally they passed beyond the farthest row and into the open. Rapidly they covered the ground toward the outposts, and nearing them, slowed down.

Then they walked forward, talking quietly among themselves, as though they were just out for an evening stroll. And then—

"Halt!" came a hoarse command.

The four obeyed. A soldier confronted them with levelled rifle.

"Who goes there?" he continued.

"Friends," was the reply.

The man peered at them closely, and still keeping them covered, raised his voice for his superior. The latter came on a dead run.

He eyed the four in the darkness and then motioned the soldier to stand back.

"It's all right," he told him.

The soldier saluted and walked away. The officer spoke to Hal.

"You are out rather late," he said.

"Right," returned the lad, "but we thought we would take a short stroll before turning in. We had no idea we had wandered so far from camp."

"Oh, it's all right," was the reply. "Who is that with you?" peering at Uncle John in the darkness.

"Just a friend we have made," said Chester, a slight tremor in his voice, for he had hoped that Uncle John's presence would be overlooked.

"I don't seem to know him," said the officer, still peering intently at Uncle John. And then suddenly he exclaimed: "The prisoner!"

He raised his voice in a cry for help; and at the same moment Hal's revolver butt crashed down upon his head!

Clair W. Hayes

CHAPTER XXV

A WILD DASH

But the damage had been done; and in response to the single wild cry, footsteps came hurrying toward them. Every sleepy outpost within hearing was wide awake now; and the alarm was carried both ways down the long battle line.

"Run!" cried Hal.

The four took to their heels and dashed ahead—in the direction that eventually would carry them into the heart of the Italian lines, were they fortunate enough to escape the bullets that in a moment would be sent whizzing after them.

"If we only had horses," thought Chester as he dashed over the ground.

The same thought struck the others, but they did not pause to give voice to it.

Fifty yards, a hundred yards they covered in the darkness before the first shot came whining after them; but this was wide, thanks to the blackness of the night. But now came a volley, from the Austrian troops behind. They could not see the running figures, but the volley was scattered and the four heard the sound of the singing bullets as they passed over their heads.

"Down!" cried Colonel Anderson, even as a second volley rang out, and they dropped just in time; for this second volley was aimed low, and would have riddled the four fugitives. A third volley passed over their prostrate forms, and then, as another did not come immediately, Colonel Anderson gave the command: "Up and on again."

This command was obeyed to the letter and again the four fugitives dashed over the ground without a word. Two, three, four hundred yards they dashed at top speed and then paused for a much needed breath and to take stock of the situation.

"Anybody hit?" asked Hal anxiously.

"No," came the reply from the other three.

"Good. Now the question is what is best to do. Undoubtedly the Austrians will send a force of cavalry out looking for our bodies, and when they fail to find them, they will spread out and give chase. That way they are bound to overtake us sooner or later. Shall we bear off to the left, with a hope of losing them, or shall we go straight ahead as fast as we can and trust to luck?"

"I think I can answer that," said Hal, suddenly. "As we came out I remember passing an old shack of some kind, a short distance off our left. I vote we make for that, and if we can reach it, we will attempt to hold it until daylight, when we can expect some assistance from the Italians. They will come to our aid when they see us besieged by the Austrians."

"A good plan," declared Colonel Anderson. "Do you think you can lead the way to the shack you speak of?"

"I can come pretty close to it," declared Hal. "My sense of direction is still with me, I believe. Come on."

Bearing slightly off to the right, he broke into a run and the others followed close behind him. For perhaps another five hundred yards, he ran forward at fair speed and then paused.

"It should be about here some place," he said. "Spread out and we'll have a look for it."

This plan was followed and a hunt for the shack began in the darkness. After perhaps five minutes, Chester's voice rang out.

"I've found it. This way."

The others made their way in the direction of his voice and a few moments later all stood before the shack.

"Is it open?" asked Chester.

Hal tried the doorknob. It was locked. Also it was barred on the outside. He put the muzzle of his revolver to the lock and would have fired had not Colonel Anderson stayed his hand.

"Hold on there," he commanded. "We don't want to open it that way if we can help it. Look around. Maybe there is a window."

At the back of the shack they found one, but it was well out of reach.

"Give me a hand up, Hal," said Chester.

Hal obeyed and Chester climbed to his shoulders. His head came level with the window. Chester pushed against it and it swung inward.

"All right," he called back. "I'm going in."

He pulled himself up and then dropped down inside. Those on the outside heard a terrible rattle and clatter and stood suddenly silent, for they did not know what had happened. Then Chester called out:

"It's all right. I jumped in the dishpan; that's all. Come on."

Hal and Colonel Anderson boosted Uncle John to the window sill, and then Hal gave Colonel Anderson a hand up. The latter, perched in the window, leaned down and pulled Hal up beside him. They dropped down inside.

At that moment a sudden beam of light flashed into the room.

The moon had come out, lighting up the outside and accentuating the darkness in the old shack.

"Well, here we are," said Chester. "Now we'll keep quiet, so as not to tell the enemy where we are."

For perhaps an hour they sat in silence; and then Hal's quick ears detected the sound of approaching horses.

"Listen!" he whispered.

The others strained their ears to catch some sound; and directly it came—the sound of many horses approaching.

"Better see to our guns," said Colonel Anderson quietly.

He examined his own brace of revolvers carefully, and Hal

and Chester did the same. Uncle John was unarmed.

"Too bad we didn't stop and get the guns of the officer I knocked down back there," said Hal. "However, it's too late now. We'll have to get along with these."

"Perhaps they won't find this place in the darkness," said Uncle John hopefully.

"Don't fool yourself there," said Chester. "They'll find it all right. That is their business, right now. Besides, it's not so dark as it was when we arrived."

"Maybe they won't take the trouble to look in," persisted Uncle John.

"They'll look in, all right," replied Hal dryly.

"Whoa!" came a voice in Austrian from outside.

Other voices became audible.

"Maybe they are in this old shack," said one.

"Hardly possible they found it in the darkness," replied another.

"We'll have a look, anyhow," declared a third.

Footsteps advanced toward the front door and a hand tried the knob.

"Locked," said a voice, "and, as you see, barred from the outside. I guess they are not in there."

"Any windows?" asked another voice.

The pursuers moved around the house.

"Here's one," exclaimed a voice, stopping before the window by which the fugitives had entered the shack.

"Climb in and have a look around," came a command.

"And get shot in the darkness?" questioned the other. "What's the matter with your doing that?"

"Afraid, eh," said the other. "Here, give me a hand up."

A moment later, in the moonlight that streamed through the window, the four inside saw the face of the first of their pursuers; but in the darkness within, the occupants of the shack were not visible.

"I can see no one," said the Austrian.

"Get down and have a look," said the other.

The man in the window drew himself up to the sill and then turned and dropped down inside; and even as he struck the floor Colonel Anderson dealt him a terrific blow over the head with the butt of a revolver.

The man fell forward on his face without so much as a groan.

Then there was silence for some minutes.

"Well," came a voice from outside, "what's the matter with you in there? Find anything?"

Hal stepped close to the window, and mimicking the first Austrian's voice, replied:

"Don't see a thing. Nobody here."

"All right then; come on out."

"I'll have a better look first," replied Hal.

"Now what good is all that going to do?" demanded Chester of Hal. "They won't go away and leave him here; and they'll discover his absence before long."

"Just a little play for time," replied Hal. "Every minute helps, you know. If we can hold out till daylight we will be all right."

"Right you are," whispered Colonel Anderson. "Minutes are precious things right now."

There was silence for a few minutes; then the voice of the man without came again:

"Say; what are you doing in there, anyhow? Are you coming out or not?"

"In a minute," mimicked Hal again.

"Find anything yet?"

"No."

"Then come on out of there, and let's go."

"All right, I'll be right out now."

Again there was silence.

A revolver butt tapped the side of the house.

"Come on out of there," said the Austrian outside.

"Coming," replied Hal.

Again silence; but this time broken from an unexpected source.

There came a sudden cry from the man on the floor—the man whom Colonel Anderson had struck down as he jumped into the room:

"Help!"

Just that one word; that was all. Again a revolver butt crashed upon the Austrian's head and he subsided without a murmur.

But the one word had given the warning.

The Austrian who had remained on the outside of the shack awaiting the return of his friend, also raised his voice.

"The fugitives are in here!" he shouted. "This way, men!"

Came the sound of many running footsteps.

"We're in for it now," said Colonel Anderson quietly. "All ready?"

"All ready," replied Hal and Chester quietly.

"Good! Take your places in the corners of the room—as much out of the line of fire as possible."

This was done.

"Surrender!" came a voice from without.

CHAPTER XXVI

FOUR AGAINST MANY

Chester could not resist the temptation to answer this demand.

"Come and get us!" he called back defiantly.

Uncle John created a slight diversion at this moment. He had been stooping over the form of the unconscious German in the shack, and now straightened up with an exclamation of satisfaction.

"Well, I've got these, anyway," he said.

He displayed a brace of revolvers and a cartridge belt which he had taken from the fallen man.

"Good," said Colonel Anderson. "Now, Hal, you and I will guard the door, and Chester and Uncle John will take care of the window. The chances are they will attack from both directions at once. Stand as far back as possible and out of the line of fire."

At that moment there came a crash against the door, as if several men were pounding upon it with their rifle butts. And this, indeed, was the case.

"Quick!" commanded Colonel Anderson. "Shove this table and these chairs against the door. Brace it with anything you can find. We should have done it sooner."

Chester and Uncle John gave up their posts guarding the window for a minute and helped in the work of barricading the entrance. And all the time the pounding continued.

As Chester stepped back after putting the last chair into place, there came a report from behind him. There was a flash that lighted up the shack like day, and the lad felt a bullet whiz past his ear.

He whirled quickly, and fired in the direction of the window, where he saw a head bobbing down. The Austrian had dodged quickly after his shot, but Chester had been quicker still; and the Austrian toppled down outside at the feet of his companions. The fall was plainly audible.

"I got one of 'em!" shouted Chester gleefully.

"Good for you," replied Hal. "We'll get the rest of them as fast as they come."

The pounding upon the door continued and the occupants of the shack kept their eyes upon it anxiously.

"It gave a little that time," declared Hal, after an extraordinarily furious blow. "It won't last much longer. Then we'll have to do some real fighting."

"They will hardly rush us," said the colonel. "We should be able to pick them off as fast as they come through. They won't try that long."

At this juncture Chester grew tired of waiting. He motioned Uncle John to give him a hand up and from the latter's shoulder raised his head cautiously to the edge of the window. For the moment he was not seen. A body of Austrians stood beneath the window, engaged in deep conversation.

Quickly Chester levelled his automatic and pressed the trigger. Ten shots struck squarely in the little knot of the enemy, and several men fell.

A cry of anger rose on the night air, as Chester leaped down within the little cabin.

"Think I got some more of 'em that time," he said with a grin. "They'll find out we can take the initiative ourselves once in a while."

"Let them alone, unless they bother us," ordered Colonel Anderson. "The longer they keep quiet and do nothing, the better for us. Time is the one factor that will work to our advantage."

"I forgot about that," returned Chester a little sheepishly.

There came a terrible thundering upon the door now; and it was evident that many men without had been called to force an entrance.

"It can't hold much longer," declared Hal quietly.

"About two more like that and it will give," agreed Colonel Anderson.

Another rain of blows was followed by a crash, as the bottom of the door gave way. A moment later it tumbled inward against the table and chairs stacked up to brace it.

And even as it did so, Colonel Anderson and Hal pressed the triggers of their revolvers. Once, twice, each spoke, and the voices of the automatics were rewarded by cries of pain from the outside.

"We must have done some damage," said Hal quietly.

Colonel Anderson did not reply; but stepping forward behind the improvised barricade, again levelled his revolver and fired twice.

"Think I got a couple that trip," he remarked.

He glanced around the room quickly.

"Back in the corners," he instructed. "They'll probably try to rush us this time."

He had predicted correctly.

For a moment there was silence without; but suddenly there came a wild yell and a score of Austrians dashed forward to force an entrance to the shack.

"Make every shot count!" cried Hal.

The occupants of the cabin waited until the foe was in plain sight and then four revolvers spoke once. As many men dropped in their tracks—for at that distance a miss was practically impossible; but the other Austrians came on.

Again four revolvers spoke; and this time only three men dropped. A third volley from the occupants of the cabin accounted for two. The Austrians hesitated.

"We're wasting bullets," declared Hal. "One is enough for

each man. Uncle John, you take the man on the far left, Chester, you the one next to him, Colonel Anderson, the third is for you. I'll take the man on this side."

"A good idea," replied the colonel. "One bullet for one Austrian. That's all each is worth."

As the Austrians, after a moment of hesitation, pressed forward once more, the weapons of the four friends spoke twice in rapid succession with greater effect.

This was enough for the enemy—for the time being, at least. They drew off and the occupants of the shack had time for a breathing spell and an opportunity to reload their weapons.

"They'll be back in a few minutes," declared Colonel Anderson. "Their officers will not let them give up as long as we are here."

"Well, we'll be ready for them," said Chester grimly.

"So we will, Chester," declared Hal. He turned to Uncle John. "Well, what do you think of this kind of a life, sir?" he asked.

Uncle John smiled faintly.

"It's not so bad," he replied. "It's a little strange to me, but you notice I have been able to fire a gun. I guess I'll get used to it in time."

"You are a brave and cool-headed man, sir," declared Colonel Anderson. "I do not believe I was half so cool my first time under fire."

"If you really knew how scared I was, you wouldn't say

that," was Uncle John's reply.

A hail from outside interrupted further talk.

"What do you suppose they want now?" asked Hal.

"Don't know," replied the colonel briefly. "We'll see." He raised his voice in a shout.

"What do you want?" he demanded in German.

"Want to have a talk with you," was the reply.

"Talk away," replied the colonel.

"We would give you a chance of life and to avoid further bloodshed," replied the Austrian.

"There has been no bloodshed in here," returned Colonel Anderson, "except among your men. We are perfectly whole and ready to fight some more."

"Then you refuse to surrender?"

"We do; most decidedly."

There was no more talk from the Austrians; neither was there another immediate attack. The quiet without became so pronounced that Hal became uneasy.

"What do you suppose they are doing?" he asked.

"Haven't any idea," replied Colonel Anderson.

"Well, you can take my word for it they are up to some mischief," declared Chester. "This silence bodes no good for us, I'll bet."

"Well, as long as they let us alone, it's a point in our favor," declared Colonel Anderson. "It is less than an hour until daylight now. Then we shall have help."

"The Austrians will have a whack at us before that," said Hal positively. "But I would like to know what's up."

"So would I," declared Chester. "And I am positive that there's something."

"I guess we'll know soon enough," said Uncle John.

And they did learn—not fifteen minutes later.

"What's that funny noise out there?" asked Chester suddenly.

The others strained their ears.

"I don't hear anything," said Hal. "You must—Wait, though. What is that noise?"

Again all listened intently. There was a faint "crack, crack," as though some one were walking upon fallen twigs.

At that moment Chester detected another cause for alarm.

"I smell smoke," he said suddenly.

"By George! that's what's the matter," shouted Hal. "They are going to smoke us out and shoot us down, or burn us here like rats in a trap. What are we going to do?" he demanded anxiously.

"Don't get excited, in the first place," replied Colonel

Anderson coolly, "We are in a ticklish situation, and that's a fact, but there must be some way out of it. Now let's see. We can't get out the front door without being shot down. The same goes for the window as the house undoubtedly is surrounded. Then what are we to do?"

"There is only one thing I can think of," declared Hal.

"And that?"

"As long as we are playing for time, stay here until we can stand it no longer because of the heat. Then make a break for it. Perhaps we can take them by surprise, grab four horses and get a good start."

"There is little chance of that," replied Colonel Anderson. "But it seems to be the only way. We'll do it."

Their plans thus made, they waited patiently, conversing in low tones, the while keeping their eyes open. The flames were crackling merrily now, and the heat was becoming intense, while occasional clouds of smoke rolled into the single room. It was too hot to remain still. Colonel Anderson spoke. "We've stood it long enough," he said. "Guns ready, and let's go!"

Clair W. Hayes

CHAPTER XXVII

A SACRIFICE

"Hold on there a minute," said Chester. "We are forgetting one thing."

"What's that?" demanded Colonel Anderson.

"Why," returned Chester, "that at least one of us must get back to General Ferrari and give him the information we were sent after."

"But how can we?"

"Well, not by jumping out there and fighting and getting killed, all of us. I've a plan."

"You'll have to hurry," said Hal. "It's getting too hot in here."

"Listen then," said Chester, speaking rapidly. "I'll climb up to this window and drop out. They won't shoot at me at first, because they naturally will think I am about to surrender. When I get to the bottom, I'll wait for either you or Colonel Anderson, as you may decide. When one of you reach my side, we'll both run. The Austrians will give chase. When I yell, the two who remain here will make a break out the door, try to find a couple of horses and head for the Italian lines. Come, now, let's get busy."

Without awaiting a reply, he crossed to the window.

"A hand up, Uncle John," he said quietly.

The latter hurried to his side, and making a step of his uncle's hand, Chester pulled himself up. A moment later he disappeared.

"I'll be the other," declared Colonel Anderson and started toward the window. Hal stretched out a hand and detained him.

"No, I'll go," he said.

"You forget," said Colonel Anderson, "that I am in command of this expedition, sir. I command you to obey my orders."

Hal stepped back.

"Very well," he said slowly.

Uncle John gave the colonel a hand up, and then hurried to Hal's side, and the two stood awaiting the word that would send them from their fiery retreat in a wild dash through the Austrian troops without.

Suddenly the sound came. Hal heard it plainly—Chester's voice, raised in a shout in English.

"All right! Go!"

With a low cry to Uncle John to follow him, Hal leaped through the scattered heap of chairs, over the table and dead bodies that almost blocked his progress, and into the open. Uncle John was right behind him.

The way seemed clear and Hal's heart beat with hope as he made out directly ahead of him the shadowy form of what he knew to be a body of horses. He dashed toward them silently.

He seized a bridle of the first horse and tossed it to Uncle John, who leaped quickly to the saddle, and waited a moment for Hal. The lad was astride a second horse a moment later and whirling the animals quickly, they urged them forward in the darkness at top speed.

At that moment a form blocked their way.

With a quick movement Hal whipped out his automatic, and without pausing to take aim, fired. The bullet went true, and the man toppled to one side even as Hal's horse would have trampled him under foot.

There came a loud cry from behind and Hal realized that their ruse had been discovered.

"Hurry," he called to Uncle John.

A volley of bullets was sent after the flying horsemen by the Austrians, who realized for the first time that two of their quarry were about to escape.

"Mount and after them," came a hoarse Austrian command.

Half a dozen troopers made a rush for their horses, while as many more dropped to their knees, levelled their rifles and fired into the darkness where the fugitives had been a moment before.

But the darkness was a blessing to the two fugitives. The Austrians were aiming by mere guess and neither rider was touched.

Hal began to breathe easier. He checked the pace a trifle, as he realized that Uncle John was lagging a little behind, his horse, apparently, not being as fresh or as swift as the one the lad bestrode.

And now the boy caught the sound of hoofbeats hurrying after them.

"Hurry, Uncle John!" he called anxiously. "They are after us."

Uncle John urged his horse to greater effort and the animal responded nobly. For a moment he kept pace with Hal's swifter mount.

Hal dropped the reins to his horse's neck, and drew his second revolver. Then he slackened the pace of his horse even more.

"Go ahead!" he cried as Uncle John flashed by. "I'll hold 'em back a minute or two."

The pursuers gained upon him. Hal stopped his horse.

A moment later the Austrians became visible in the now semi-darkness—for dawn was breaking. Hal raised both weapons and fired three times in rapid succession.

His effort was rewarded by several cries of pain from the pursuers, and the others checked their horses abruptly. Again Hal fired twice; and then, turning his horse quickly, rode swiftly after Uncle John.

The Austrians hesitated a moment before again taking up the chase, and this brief moment was the time the fugitives needed.

As they galloped along, Hal still somewhat in the rear, it grew light and less than a half a mile ahead the riders made out the first Italian outpost. They headed toward it with loud cries, the Austrians now again in pursuit.

Their cries were heard in the Italian lines, and quicker than it takes to tell it, Hal's heart was made glad by the sight of a mounted squadron of Italian troops dashing toward them.

He slowed his horse down to a walk, and turning in the saddle, took a parting shot at the Austrians, who now had turned to flee. One threw up his arms, and dropped to the ground, and the horse went on riderless.

The Italian horsemen pulled up when they reached Hal's side, and the lad explained the situation in a few words.

"If you are quick," he told the officer, "you may take them unaware and rescue my two companions."

The officer wasted no time in words; a quick command to his men, and the troop went on in pursuit of the foe.

Hal turned to Uncle John.

"There is nothing we can do for them," he said. "We shall go to General Ferrari and make our report."

He led the way, more slowly now.

The Italian commander received them immediately and Hal gave him the information they had gained in as few words as possible. After receiving the thanks of the general, the boy, followed by Uncle John, again made his way to the front; and at the extreme outpost, saw the Italians who had pursued the Austrians returning—empty-handed.

The officer greeted him with a gesture of sorrow.

"It was no use," he said. "They had started when we reached there. We pursued them as far as advisable, and fell back only when a strong force of the enemy came out to meet us."

Hal thanked him and with Uncle John returned to his quarters, seeking to think of some way by which he could be of service to his chum and to Colonel Anderson.

Meanwhile, what of the other two?

When Chester leaped from the burning shack, he awaited the arrival of the next, who proved to be Colonel Anderson, even as he had planned. As Chester had figured, the Austrians did not attack him when he reached the ground, evidently believing he was about to surrender.

A moment later Colonel Anderson stood beside him, and as the latter raised himself to his feet, Chester shouted the words that had set Hal and Uncle John on their dash for life:

"All right! Go!"

At these words, he and Colonel Anderson also dashed ahead. Taken by the surprise, the Austrians hesitated a moment and then dashed after them with cries. The men who had been guarding the door by which Hal and Uncle John later escaped, also joined in the chase.

For a couple of seconds the Austrians did not fire at the

Clair W. Hayes

fugitives, evidently believing they could catch them. But as the two gradually drew away from them an officer gave the command:

"Fire!"

A score of rifles cracked, but fortunately for Chester and Colonel Anderson, none of the soldiers had taken time to aim carefully. But one bullet whistled close to Chester's head.

"I can't see any use getting killed," he muttered to himself.

Colonel Anderson also came to a stop, and both raised their hands in token of surrender.

An Austrian officer advanced toward them—and he proved to be the same man with whom they had talked just before making their dash from the Austrian lines—the man whom they had knocked unconscious as he gave the alarm.

"So we have you at last, eh?" he said harshly.

"Yes, we're here," agreed Chester with a smile.

"And this time you will not get away," was the response. "Spies, eh?"

"Well, what of it?" demanded Chester.

"Nothing," replied the officer, "except that you will be shot some time to-day."

"Oh, well, that's the chance we all take," replied Chester calmly.

At this moment a subordinate approached the officer.

"The other two fugitives, sir, have taken two horses and fled," he said.

"What?" shouted the Austrian.

"Yes, sir."

The officer whirled upon Chester and Colonel Anderson.

"So," he exclaimed. "This is some more of your work. You shall pay for it."

"Perhaps," said Chester.

The officer made no reply to this. Instead he motioned them to move ahead of him, which they did. A moment later they found themselves in the saddle and headed back toward the Austrian lines, closely surrounded by their guards.

"And now," said Chester, "for another call on our friend, the general."

CHAPTER XXVIII

MR. STUBBS ONCE MORE

A hearty hand slapped Hal on the back, and he looked up from a moody reverie into the face of Anthony Stubbs.

"Well, well, what's the matter now?" demanded the little war correspondent.

"Matter enough," replied Hal. "The Austrians have nabbed Chester."

"You don't say!" exclaimed Stubbs. "I thought you fellows had finished your fighting days."

"So we had," returned the lad; "but we took one little fling, and this is the result."

"And what are you going to do about it?"

"That's what I have been trying to figure out."

"Well, I guess they won't hurt Chester any," said Stubbs.

"That's where you are wrong," declared Hal, getting to his feet. "They'll just about stand him up and shoot him as a spy."

Stubbs became more serious at once; for before he had not realized that Chester was in any immediate danger.

"As serious as all that?" he questioned. "Tell me about it. What have you fellows been up to?"

Rapidly Hal laid the facts before him.

"H-m-m," muttered Stubbs, when the lad concluded. "Chester certainly has got himself into a mess. And Anderson is with him, eh? Well, we will have to do something—and that at once."

"Yes; but what?" demanded Hal anxiously.

"Well, now, that's the question, but you'll have to give me time. I'll find a way. A newspaper man always finds a way."

Hal felt a little relieved. He couldn't see that there was the slightest chance to be of assistance to his chum, but the little war correspondent's words cheered him.

"Yep, you'll have to give me a little time," said Stubbs. "Now you wait here until I come back, and if I don't come back with a first class plan I hope to never write another story for the *Gazette*."

He walked rapidly away, leaving Hal alone with his thoughts. Fifteen minutes later the little man returned.

"All right," he said. "Let's go."

"Go?" exclaimed Hal. "Go where?"

"Why, go and get Chester and Anderson out of the hole. Are you ready?"

"Oh, I'm ready enough," replied Hal, as he fell in step and hurried along beside Stubbs, "but tell me—"

"Now hold on there," interrupted Stubbs. "I'll tell you, but I am a-going to do it in my own way. Don't hurry me."

Hal made no reply, and after a few moments the war correspondent continued:

"Yep, we'll get 'em all right—that is, if the Austrians don't beat us to it. Sure we'll get 'em."

He grew silent again, and although Hal could hardly restrain his impatience, he pressed his lips close together and said nothing. Stubbs gazed at him and smiled.

"You'll do," he said. "Now that you have managed to get a tight rein on your impatience I'll tell you. In the first place, we'll have to hurry; but first we'll turn in here a minute."

He turned abruptly to the right, and a moment later led the way into his own temporary quarters.

"My diggings, as the British say," he declared with a wave of his hands. "I'll have you fixed up in a minute."

"Fixed up?" questioned Hal.

"Sure. You didn't expect to go back to the Austrian side looking like that, did you? They'd nab you in a minute."

He rummaged among some things in a corner, and directly produced an extra suit of clothes.

"Climb into these," he ordered.

Hal did as commanded and awaited further instructions.

Stubbs opened a little box, which gave forth a peculiar smell and had a queer blackish appearance. Stubbs dipped his fingers in the box, and then passed them over Hal's face.

"Lucky I had a little experience in the art of stagecraft," he remarked as he continued the operation.

He stepped back and surveyed Hal critically.

"There," he exclaimed. "Your own mother wouldn't know you. You look all of ten years older. Got your guns?"

Hal picked them up from where he had thrown them when he had changed clothes.

"All ready," he said quietly.

"Wait till I fix myself up a little," said Stubbs. "You must remember I was within the Austrian lines not so long ago myself. They may be looking for me, too."

He again delved into the little box, and Hal, as he watched, was surprised at the change in the appearance of the man. He, too, seemed to have aged greatly, and he bore slight resemblance to the old Stubbs.

"All ready to move now," he said at last.

He led the way from his quarters, and perhaps a hundred yards away, indicated a pair of horses.

"Ours—for the journey," he said.

A moment later both were in the saddle and were riding

toward the front.

"Now," said Stubbs, "I'll resume my little talk."

"One minute," broke in Hal. "How do you figure we are going to be allowed the freedom of the Austrian camp? What'll they do with us when we get there?"

"True," said Stubbs. He reached in his pocket and produced two papers, one of which he passed to Hal. "This may help a little," he explained.

Hal looked at the paper. He found it was made out in the name of John Lawrence and that it purported to be an identification of John Lawrence as an accredited correspondent of the New York *Gazette*.

"I've got two or three more back there," said Stubbs, waving an arm in the general direction of his quarters. "They have often come in handy."

"I see," said Hal. "Then these papers are what you are figuring on to gain us the freedom of the Austrian lines."

"Freedom to a certain extent, yes," replied Stubbs. "Now for the other part of my plan. To be perfectly frank, you know just as much about it as I do. I have no plan beside getting in the Austrian lines. Events must shape themselves after that."

"But do you suppose these papers will satisfy the Austrian commander?"

"They will after I have talked to him for five minutes."

"I hope so," said Hal.

They had now passed the Italian outposts, unmolested, and rode across the open toward the Austrian lines. Some time later they were halted by an Austrian sentinel.

"Take us to the general," commanded Stubbs.

The sentinel eyed the little man aggressively, but, evidently being impressed with his manner, called a superior. To him Stubbs gave the same command, and he gave it in such a way that the officer, after a slight hesitation, turned on his heel and motioned Hal and Stubbs to follow him.

Five minutes later they stood again in the presence of General Brentz. Stubbs produced his paper and Hal did likewise. The general scanned them closely.

"How do I know you are what you represent yourselves to be?" he demanded gruffly.

"For one reason, general," said Stubbs, "because we wouldn't be here otherwise. Of course we don't expect the freedom of your lines, but we would like to know a little about the Austrian troops—whether they can fight, how they stand up under fire—what kind of men they are. The people of America want to know, and that's what we are here for."

The general hesitated.

"I've had some trouble with spies here lately," he said at length, "and I have become wary." He scrutinized them closely. "But you look honest. I'll take a chance on you. Besides, it would be well for the people of America to know something of the Austrians besides what they read from an enemy source."

"Thank you, general," said Stubbs, "and you will provide us

Clair W. Hayes

with papers so that we will not be molested?"

"Yes, I'll do that."

The general scribbled a few lines on two sheets of paper, which he passed to Stubbs. The latter gave one to Hal, and turned to go, Hal following him. At the entrance Stubbs turned quickly.

"Oh, by the way, general, about these spies—are they Italians?"

"No, they are British," was the reply.

"And there is no doubt they are spies?"

"None; they aided a prisoner to escape and were only captured after great trouble. There were two more whom we did not get."

"Oh! In that case, I suppose you will have to shoot them," Stubbs stated as a matter of fact.

"Exactly. They will be executed at sunrise to-morrow."

"In the meantime they are likely to escape again," said Stubbs.

"Not much," declared the general. He walked to the window, and pointed to a large tent a short distance away.

"See that tent?" he questioned.

Hal and Stubbs indicated that they did.

"They are confined in there," said the general, "and they are heavily guarded. I have stationed a guard of five armed men, with instructions never to leave them alone. I shall take no chances; and in the morning they shall be shot. This is no place for spies."

"I can see that, general," replied Stubbs. "Well, we are obliged to you for your courtesy, and we shall make it clear to the American people that the Austrians are not as black as they have been painted."

The general bowed courteously, and Hal and Stubbs left his quarters.

"You see," said Stubbs when they were outside, "it wasn't such a hard matter after all."

"And to think," said Hal, "that, in view of his recent experiences, he was so unwary as to betray where Chester and Colonel Anderson are confined."

"Which was lucky for us," declared Stubbs. "It will save us a lot of worry and search."

"Now what?" demanded Hal.

"Well," was the reply, "I should say that there is nothing that can be done before dark. However, we might as well take a look at the prison tent from the outside. It is always well to know the lay of the land."

Accordingly they turned their footsteps in that direction, and walked by the tent slowly. And from the inside they heard the sound of Chester's laugh, as he talked to Colonel Anderson.

"He's not worrying any, that boy," said Stubbs with a smile.

"We'll get them out safely."

All the afternoon the two prowled about the camp; and at last darkness fell. It was time to get busy, for whatever was done must be accomplished before the break of day, when a firing squad would snuff out the lives of the two prisoners.

"Well, here we go," said Stubbs.

He led the way slowly toward the prison tent.

CHAPTER XXIX

SENTENCED TO DIE

Chester's and Lieutenant Anderson's interview with General Brentz was far from being the pleasant few minutes that Hal and Stubbs had experienced. Hal now considered the general a pleasant middle-aged man and a courteous gentleman; Chester looked upon him almost as a barbarian.

General Brentz was striding wrathfully up and down his quarters when Chester and Colonel Anderson were taken before him. He greeted their arrival with a fierce scowl and motioned the guards outside the door with an angry gesture.

"So!" he exclaimed. "You are British spies instead of German secret agents, eh? Well, we know how to treat all such here. What have you to say for yourselves?"

"Nothing," said Colonel Anderson, replying for both.

"'Twould do you no good," responded the officer. "But there is one thing I would know. How does it come that you are familiar with the password of the Wilhelmstrasse?"

"I can't see where it would do any good to tell you, general," replied Chester.

"But I demand to know."

"You'll never learn from me," declared the lad.

Colonel Anderson smiled.

"That goes for me, too," he said quietly.

The general glared wrathfully at first one and then the other.

"Very well," he said, controlling his anger. "You shall both be shot at sunrise."

He gazed at the two closely to see what effect his words had; but if he expected to find an expression of fear upon either face, he was disappointed. Colonel Anderson and Chester eyed him steadily, though neither spoke.

It was what they had expected.

After a few moments the general spoke again, this time more kindly, with his eyes full upon Chester.

"You," he said, "appear to be too young for this sort of business. How do you happen to be mixed up in such desperate work?"

"It's too long a story to go into, general," replied Chester quietly. "Besides, as we have not much longer to live, Colonel Anderson and I would rather be left to ourselves."

The general seemed about to make an angry reply; then changed his mind, and asked:

"Are you English?"

"No, I am not," replied Chester. "I am an American."

"I thought so," declared the general. "Well, it's too bad, but if you will mix up in business that does not concern you, you must pay the penalty. Orderly!"

His orderly entered and came to attention.

"Have these prisoners closely confined," was the command. "Station a detail of five men and see that they are not unguarded a single moment. Then present my compliments to Colonel Frestung and tell him to have a firing squad ready at sunrise. These men are spies and must die."

Again the orderly saluted and motioned the prisoners to precede him from the general's quarters.

With heads erect and shoulders squared, Chester and Colonel Anderson marched out ahead of him. Each realized the futility of a break for liberty and each was determined to live his last moments and die the death of a soldier.

Outside a squad of soldiers surrounded them and they were led to a large tent, which was to be their last prison. Inside they found comfortable chairs, a table and several books.

"They seem to take pains to make it pleasant for a man about to die," remarked Colonel Anderson. "We should be able to spend a profitable day."

"So we should," was the reply. "I wonder if Hal and Uncle John got through safely?" he remarked somewhat irrelevantly.

"I guess we can bank on that," said the colonel. "They got through if there was a possible chance."

"I hope that Hal does not venture into the Austrian lines in an attempt to rescue us," declared Chester. "It would be sticking his head into the lion's mouth."

"Nevertheless, that is what he is likely to do," asserted Colonel Anderson. "It is not like him to keep quiet when some one is in danger."

"That's what worries me," confessed Chester. "There is no use of his being killed, too."

"Oh, well," said the colonel, "whatever happens is beyond our power to remedy. Let's talk about something pleasant."

And so they did, whiling away the rapidly flying hours with stories and reminiscences; and the shadows deepened as darkness approached.

"It seems to me that we could get out of this place some way," declared Chester suddenly.

"It seems to me that you are wrong," said, the colonel grimly. "There are five guards outside, each armed to the teeth. What chance would we have?"

"Well, I don't know," confessed Chester. "I was just thinking."

"Think while you have a chance," said the colonel with a slight grin. "Looks like our thinking days were about over."

Chester's eyes roamed about the tent. His eyes sparkled.

"We might as well have a little fun, anyhow," he remarked. "How hard do you think you could hit a man with that chair you are sitting on?"

Colonel Anderson felt the chair carefully with his fingers.

"Well, pretty hard, I guess," was his reply. "What's the idea?"

"Think you could hit him so hard he wouldn't have time to cry out?"

"Yes; if I was particular how I handled it."

"Well, we'll have a try at it then," declared Chester.

"Try at what? What do you mean?"

"I'll tell you. I'll step out of the tent. The first guard in sight will order me to get back inside. I'll protest. Then he'll put me in. When he lets loose of me, you whack him over the head with that chair, and be careful how you do it."

"Yes, but the other guards?"

"I guess we can work that all right. I have noticed that no two of the guards are in front of the tent at the same time— they are walking around all the time. When you have disposed of the first man, we'll work the same trick on the other."

"And then what?"

"Why then," said Chester simply, "we'll put on their uniforms and walk out of here."

"By Jove!" ejaculated the colonel. "Now I wonder—"

He broke off and for some moments was lost in thought. Then he got quietly to his feet, determination written upon his strong features.

"It may work," he said. "We'll try it. But we'll have to move quickly and silently; and we shall have to don the uniforms almost in a single jump."

"All right," said Chester. "Ready?"

"All ready," replied the colonel with a nod.

He picked up the heavy chair and swung it once about his head. Then he took up a position at the side of the tent, just out of view from the entrance.

Chester walked boldly from the tent.

"Get back in there," came a harsh command in Austrian.

Chester paid no heed and continued to gaze straight ahead into the rapidly descending darkness.

"Get back in there," came the command, and still Chester made no move.

The Austrian soldier came up to the lad, and taking him by the shoulders, thrust him within the tent. Chester threw out an arm and succeeded in drawing the man in after him. Then he released his own hold, and with an effort shook off the grip of his captor. At the same moment he jumped lightly aside and called in a hoarse whisper:

"Now!"

There was a rush of air as the heavy chair descended, followed by a dull thud, and a second impact as the soldier fell to the ground with a crushed skull. Colonel Anderson was over the unconscious form in a moment, ready to choke an outcry should his blow not have been true. But there was no need for this. His aim had been true, and the man was unconscious before he fell.

"All right," whispered the colonel hoarsely. "Rip off your clothes while I get him out of this uniform."

Chester flung off his clothes hurriedly, and stepped quickly into the uniform Colonel Anderson gave him. Then he deprived the man of his gun and revolvers.

"All ready for the next one," he said. He moved toward the door.

"Hold on there," called the colonel. "You can't go in that uniform."

"By George! you're right," declared Chester. "What now?"

"You'll have to wield the chair," was the reply. "There is no time to change again."

He walked out of the tent and Chester picked up the chair and stepped into position.

This time, therefore, it was Colonel Anderson who engaged in a heated altercation with a second Austrian soldier. The plan worked as well as before and the man pushed the colonel back into the tent. The latter dragged the man in after him and stepped hurriedly aside, just as Chester brought the chair down upon the Austrian's defenseless head with all his power. The man dropped like a log.

Hurriedly Colonel Anderson stripped off his outer garments and climbed into the Austrian's uniform. Then he seized the man's gun and revolvers and led the way from the tent.

"If you see another of them, keep your back toward him if possible," whispered the colonel.

And just as Chester emerged from the tent a third guard stepped around the side. Chester turned his back, as did Colonel Anderson, and the man paid no heed to them. The fugitives walked away quickly.

Out of sight of the tent they slowed down and breathed with relief.

"Which way now?" asked Chester.

"As straight toward the front as we can go," was the reply. "We'll have to trust to luck to get through."

They made off with all speed.

And suddenly, from the direction in which they had come, there came a loud cry, followed by several pistol shots and the sound of footsteps running after them.

"They have discovered our escape!" shouted Colonel Anderson. "Run."

He suited the action to the word and Chester ran after him.

"We'd better double back and try to throw them off our track," called the colonel over his shoulder.

He swerved to the right, ran a few rods, and turned to the right again.

And then, abruptly, he came to a pause. Chester, a step behind, crashed into him. He stumbled, and uttered an exclamation of dismay, as he heard Colonel

Anderson say:

"We surrender!"

Clair W. Hayes

CHAPTER XXX

SAFE

As Hal and Anthony Stubbs approached the tent in which Chester and Colonel Anderson had been so recently confined, they discussed their plan of action; and after several plans had been advanced and rejected, Hal decided that caution must be thrown to the winds.

"A quick dash—and a fight if necessary," he declared.

And Stubbs had agreed, peaceful man though he was; and although Hal did not know it, the little man was literally shaking in his boots. However, like many men of his kind, he had a certain manner of concealing his nervousness, and he now followed Hal coolly enough.

Fifty yards from the tent Hal paused, as he saw two figures emerge from the prison and walk quickly away.

"Strange. Wonder what that means?" he said to himself. He turned to Stubbs. "All right now," he said quietly. "Follow me and be quick."

He ran lightly forward and dashed into the tent. And in the darkness he stumbled over a prostrate form. Quickly he drew a match from his pocket and struck, it. The face of the man on the floor was not that of Chester nor Colonel Anderson. The flare of the match showed him a second prostrate form, and he saw that this, too, was a stranger to him. Then he saw the discarded clothing and realized what had transpired.

"Quick, Stubbs! They have escaped!" he shouted, and darted from the tent.

And in the entrance he met an Austrian guard, whose attention had been attracted by the sound of Hal stumbling within. The man uttered a low exclamation and sought to bring his gun to bear.

But Hal was too quick for him. In spite of the fact that he keenly realized the need of caution, he also realized the value of time. His hand slipped quickly to his revolver, and without raising it he fired from his hip. The Austrian staggered back and tumbled over.

"We're in for it!" cried Hal. "Follow me and hurry!"

He dashed forward in the direction recently taken by the two figures he had seen leave the tent, for he felt sure the forms were those of Chester and Colonel Anderson.

Stubbs was right behind him. Fear lent wings to the little man's legs, and Hal, despite his longer strides, did not forge ahead of him. Both ran at full speed.

And suddenly Hal made out figures in front, and before he could swerve aside, he heard Colonel Anderson's well-known voice exclaim:

"We surrender!"

Clair W. Hayes

With a stifled shout, Hal put forth an extra burst of speed, as he realized that the men who held the drop on Chester and Colonel Anderson numbered but three, although from beyond he could see others rushing toward them.

Again his revolver spoke and a bullet whizzed close to Colonel Anderson's head; but an Austrian soldier dropped. The others were taken by surprise, and relaxed their vigilance for a moment. And then Colonel Anderson and Chester, who had now recovered his balance, fired.

Chester started as he recognized Hal's voice, which now called out:

"Quick, Chester! To the right."

Colonel Anderson was no less surprised, but he did not hesitate; and closely bunched the four turned to the right and ran for their lives.

Men sprang up on all sides now; and it seemed impossible that the four could escape. But fortune favored them.

Swerving suddenly again, Hal, who was in the lead, stopped short, and uttered a cry of pure dismay. The way ahead was blocked. There seemed no way out; and then Chester cried:

"An aeroplane hangar!"

It was true. Fortune had guided their footsteps to possibly the only place in the whole Austrian camp where there was a chance of escape.

Hal wasted no time. Rapidly he mounted the hangar, the others following him closely. The lad uttered a short prayer as he climbed and then gave a great sigh of relief. He had feared there would be no air craft there, but, and Hal cried his relief aloud, there was.

He glanced at the machine quickly and uttered another cry of joy as he made out that the craft was exceptionally large, capable of seating at least ten men, and the additional fact that it was a self starter.

"Climb in quick!" he shouted, leaping into the pilot's seat and taking the wheel.

The others followed this command with all despatch, and Chester took his place at the motor.

"Let 'er go, Chester!" shouted Hal.

There came a faint buzz at first, followed by a louder noise as the motor began to whir; there was the sound of the whizzing propellers, and the machine shot from the hangar with a lurch.

And at the same moment there came from all sides volleys of rifle and pistol shots. Chester felt a sharp tinge in his left arm, and Hal felt the breeze of a bullet as it flew by his ear. Colonel Anderson was untouched, but Stubbs sent up a howl of anguish.

"I'm shot!" he cried and started to his feet.

The machine rocked crazily as he attempted to rise and Colonel Anderson reached quickly up and seized him by the arm.

"Sit down, you fool!" he commanded. "Do you want to spill us all out?"

Hal threw over the elevating lever and the huge air craft soared into the sky. And not until they had reached an altitude of a thousand feet did Hal straighten the machine out for a level flight.

Then he slowed down a moment to take stock of injuries.

"Hit, Colonel Anderson?" he asked.

"No," was the reply.

"You, Chester?"

"Scratch, I guess," answered Chester. "Bullet touched me on the arm. Doesn't amount to much."

"Stubbs?" queried Hal.

"I'm killed!" exclaimed the little man, and there was the trace of a quaver in his voice. "Shot through the heart."

"Nonsense!" exclaimed Hal. "If you had been shot through the heart you wouldn't be talking about it now."

"But I was," protested Stubbs.

"Look him over, Colonel Anderson," instructed Hal. "If it's as bad as all that, throw him out. We can't be bothered with excess now."

"No! No! I'm all right!" declared Stubbs, drawing away as Colonel Anderson extended an exploring hand. "I don't think the bullet touched me."

"All right then," declared Hal, smiling to himself, for his ruse had worked. "We'll go ahead then."

"Which way?" demanded Chester.

"Back to the Italian lines; and it behooves us to hurry. There will be a squadron of the enemy after us in a minute."

"Right," declared Chester briefly.

But, much as they would have liked it, they were not to get back within the heart of the Italian army for many a long day; and strenuous times were to befall them before they again saw their mothers, and Uncle John, who was to put in many weary days searching for them.

As Hal headed the huge machine southward, a blinding glare caught his eyes. It cut off his view entirely, and only for the lad's quick wit, might have ended the lives of all.

But the moment the light blinded him Hal acted. He knew in an instant from whence it came, and he swerved to the right so quickly as almost to upset the plane; but it was in time to avoid the forward sweep of an enemy plane.

"Wow!" cried Stubbs. "Don't throw me out!"

"Keep quiet," ordered Hal, when he had slowed down a bit, so as to ease his dazzled eyes and gain his bearings.

"What was the matter?" demanded Chester.

"Matter?" echoed Hal. "You mean to tell me you didn't see that other airship flash by?"

"I didn't," replied Chester.

"Well, I did," declared Hal. "We'll have to get away from here pretty quick. There'll be more of them along in a minute."

He threw over the elevating lever and the craft soared higher into the heavens. And again Hal turned south.

Once more he caught the flash of a hostile craft in time to avoid being run down. Again and again it happened. And at last Hal said:

"Evidently there is no use trying to get back that way. They must be on the lookout for us. What shall we do?"

"Whatever you say," replied Chester.

"We'll take a vote on it," Hal decided. "I'll make my suggestion first."

"All right," was the reply.

"Then I'll suggest that we head in some other direction and keep going until we have passed out of the enemy's territory."

"Which way?" asked Colonel Anderson.

Hal considered a few minutes before replying.

"Well," he said finally, "I should say east."

"What!" exclaimed Chester. "Right into the heart of Austria?"

"And why not?" Hal wanted to know. "We'll be safer there than any place else. Besides, if we go far enough we'll eventually land in Greece or perhaps Servia or Montenegro.

They won't be expecting a foe that far from Italian soil. What do you say, Colonel Anderson?"

"I'm with you," was the quiet response. "I believe that is good reasoning."

"My only objection," said Chester, "is that we must get back to Uncle John, and then to Rome, where mother is."

"True," replied Hal. "But mother would a great deal rather have us safe in Greece or Servia, than dead in Italy."

"Which is more good reasoning," declared Colonel Anderson.

"I guess you are right," replied Chester. "I'm with you then."

"And you, Stubbs?" questioned Hal. "You have a vote on this."

"Oh my, I don't care where you go," was the answer in a weak voice, "just so you let me put my feet on the ground once more. I'm so sick."

"Poor fellow," said Chester, in a low voice, "he's frightened."

"What's that?" demanded Stubbs in a shrill voice.

"Frightened? Me frightened? I'll leave it to Hal there if I am frightened. Who was it found the way to get here and help you fellows, anyhow? Who was it, I ask you? I'll tell you who it was. It was me, Anthony Stubbs, war correspondent of the New York *Gazette*. Yes, sir, it was—Oh, let's go down. I'm so sick."

"Stubbs, you are all right," declared Hal, and added to the

others: "What he says is perfectly true. Had it not been for him, we would not be here now. He conceived the plan that admitted us to the Austrian lines, and if it were light enough you would see that it was a good plan. I'll venture to say you would know neither one of us but for our voices," and he explained in detail.

"By George, Mr. Stubbs, I didn't think you had it in you!" exclaimed Chester. He stretched forth a hand. "Shake!" he said.

"Oh, please let me alone," moaned Stubbs. "I'm terribly sick. How long before we can go down?"

"Not for some hours, I'm afraid," replied Hal. "If we were to descend now we would fall into the hands of the Austrians."

"I don't care whose hands we fall into," mumbled Stubbs, "if we could only fall, that's all I ask."

"He must be sick," declared Chester. "Funny it never affected me that way."

"No, it's not," declared Stubbs, suddenly taking an interest in things. "Nothing would affect you like it does me. Nor any of the rest of you. You are hardened to these things. I'm a man of peace, and sympathetic, and kind. You are a lot of hard-hearted brutes."

The other three occupants of the machine smiled to themselves. Not for the world would they have laughed at the little man, for he was very close to them all. And at last Hal said:

"Tell you what, Stubbs. I'll put on a little extra speed, just for your benefit. We'll get you back on terra firma just as soon as we can."

Stubbs' only reply was another moan.

"Well, Chester," said Hal, "here we are again, flying over an enemy's country. May we be as fortunate as we have been before."

"Which we shall be," was Chester's quiet response. "We have had our share of bad luck in the last few days. Fortune must smile on us at last."

And Chester proved himself a true prophet; for, before another sun had risen and set, the huge air craft had carried its four occupants safely across the Austrian empire and beyond the Montenegrin border. And here, among these hardy mountaineers, among the best fighters in the world—among the people of this little Balkan kingdom—the smallest to declare war against the Teuton oppressor—the lads were to see more of the horrors of war—were again to play active parts in the struggle. And also they were to see service with the heroic Servian troops, than whom there are none braver.

But these adventures must come in their proper place; and so, for the time, we must again take leave of these two lads and their brave companions and friends, but only to meet them again in a succeeding volume, entitled: "The Boy Allies in the Balkan Campaign; or The Struggle to Save a Nation."

Choose from Thousands of 1stWorldLibrary Classics By

A. M. Barnard
Ada Leverson
Adolphus William Ward
Aesop
Agatha Christie
Alexander Aaronsohn
Alexander Kielland
Alexandre Dumas
Alfred Gatty
Alfred Ollivant
Alice Duer Miller
Alice Turner Curtis
Alice Dunbar
Allen Chapman
Alleyne Ireland
Ambrose Bierce
Amelia E. Barr
Amory H. Bradford
Andrew Lang
Andrew McFarland Davis
Andy Adams
Angela Brazil
Anna Alice Chapin
Anna Sewell
Annie Besant
Annie Hamilton Donnell
Annie Payson Call
Annie Roe Carr
Annonaymous
Anton Chekhov
Archibald Lee Fletcher
Arnold Bennett
Arthur C. Benson
Arthur Conan Doyle
Arthur M. Winfield
Arthur Ransome
Arthur Schnitzler
Arthur Train
Atticus
B.H. Baden-Powell
B. M. Bower
B. C. Chatterjee
Baroness Emmuska Orczy
Baroness Orczy
Basil King
Bayard Taylor
Ben Macomber
Bertha Muzzy Bower
Bjornstjerne Bjornson

Booth Tarkington
Boyd Cable
Bram Stoker
C. Collodi
C. E. Orr
C. M. Ingleby
Carolyn Wells
Catherine Parr Traill
Charles A. Eastman
Charles Amory Beach
Charles Dickens
Charles Dudley Warner
Charles Farrar Browne
Charles Ives
Charles Kingsley
Charles Klein
Charles Hanson Towne
Charles Lathrop Pack
Charles Romyn Dake
Charles Whibley
Charles Willing Beale
Charlotte M. Braeme
Charlotte M. Yonge
Charlotte Perkins Stetson
Clair W. Hayes
Clarence Day Jr.
Clarence E. Mulford
Clemence Housman
Confucius
Coningsby Dawson
Cornelis DeWitt Wilcox
Cyril Burleigh
D. H. Lawrence
Daniel Defoe
David Garnett
Dinah Craik
Don Carlos Janes
Donald Keyhoe
Dorothy Kilner
Dougan Clark
Douglas Fairbanks
E. Nesbit
E. P. Roe
E. Phillips Oppenheim
E. S. Brooks
Earl Barnes
Edgar Rice Burroughs
Edith Van Dyne
Edith Wharton

Edward Everett Hale
Edward J. O'Biren
Edward S. Ellis
Edwin L. Arnold
Eleanor Atkins
Eleanor Hallowell Abbott
Eliot Gregory
Elizabeth Gaskell
Elizabeth McCracken
Elizabeth Von Arnim
Ellem Key
Emerson Hough
Emilie F. Carlen
Emily Bronte
Emily Dickinson
Enid Bagnold
Enilor Macartney Lane
Erasmus W. Jones
Ernie Howard Pie
Ethel May Dell
Ethel Turner
Ethel Watts Mumford
Eugene Sue
Eugenie Foa
Eugene Wood
Eustace Hale Ball
Evelyn Everett-green
Everard Cotes
F. H. Cheley
F. J. Cross
F. Marion Crawford
Fannie E. Newberry
Federick Austin Ogg
Ferdinand Ossendowski
Fergus Hume
Florence A. Kilpatrick
Fremont B. Deering
Francis Bacon
Francis Darwin
Frances Hodgson Burnett
Frances Parkinson Keyes
Frank Gee Patchin
Frank Harris
Frank Jewett Mather
Frank L. Packard
Frank V. Webster
Frederic Stewart Isham
Frederick Trevor Hill
Frederick Winslow Taylor

Friedrich Kerst
Friedrich Nietzsche
Fyodor Dostoyevsky
G.A. Henty
G.K. Chesterton
Gabrielle E. Jackson
Garrett P. Serviss
Gaston Leroux
George A. Warren
George Ade
Geroge Bernard Shaw
George Cary Eggleston
George Durston
George Ebers
George Eliot
George Gissing
George MacDonald
George Meredith
George Orwell
George Sylvester Viereck
George Tucker
George W. Cable
George Wharton James
Gertrude Atherton
Gordon Casserly
Grace E. King
Grace Gallatin
Grace Greenwood
Grant Allen
Guillermo A. Sherwell
Gulielma Zollinger
Gustav Flaubert
H. A. Cody
H. B. Irving
H. C. Bailey
H. G. Wells
H. H. Munro
H. Irving Hancock
H. R. Naylor
H. Rider Haggard
H. W. C. Davis
Haldeman Julius
Hall Caine
Hamilton Wright Mabie
Hans Christian Andersen
Harold Avery
Harold McGrath
Harriet Beecher Stowe
Harry Castlemon
Harry Coghill
Harry Houidini

Hayden Carruth
Helent Hunt Jackson
Helen Nicolay
Hendrik Conscience
Hendy David Thoreau
Henri Barbusse
Henrik Ibsen
Henry Adams
Henry Ford
Henry Frost
Henry James
Henry Jones Ford
Henry Seton Merriman
Henry W Longfellow
Herbert A. Giles
Herbert Carter
Herbert N. Casson
Herman Hesse
Hildegard G. Frey
Homer
Honore De Balzac
Horace B. Day
Horace Walpole
Horatio Alger Jr.
Howard Pyle
Howard R. Garis
Hugh Lofting
Hugh Walpole
Humphry Ward
Ian Maclaren
Inez Haynes Gillmore
Irving Bacheller
Isabel Cecilia Williams
Isabel Hornibrook
Israel Abrahams
Ivan Turgenev
J. G.Austin
J. Henri Fabre
J. M. Barrie
J. M. Walsh
J. Macdonald Oxley
J. R. Miller
J. S. Fletcher
J. S. Knowles
J. Storer Clouston
J. W. Duffield
Jack London
Jacob Abbott
James Allen
James Andrews
James Baldwin

James Branch Cabell
James DeMille
James Joyce
James Lane Allen
James Lane Allen
James Oliver Curwood
James Oppenheim
James Otis
James R. Driscoll
Jane Abbott
Jane Austen
Jane L. Stewart
Janet Aldridge
Jens Peter Jacobsen
Jerome K. Jerome
Jessie Graham Flower
John Buchan
John Burroughs
John Cournos
John F. Kennedy
John Gay
John Glasworthy
John Habberton
John Joy Bell
John Kendrick Bangs
John Milton
John Philip Sousa
John Taintor Foote
Jonas Lauritz Idemil Lie
Jonathan Swift
Joseph A. Altsheler
Joseph Carey
Joseph Conrad
Joseph E. Badger Jr
Joseph Hergesheimer
Joseph Jacobs
Jules Vernes
Julian Hawthrone
Julie A Lippmann
Justin Huntly McCarthy
Kakuzo Okakura
Karle Wilson Baker
Kate Chopin
Kenneth Grahame
Kenneth McGaffey
Kate Langley Bosher
Kate Langley Bosher
Katherine Cecil Thurston
Katherine Stokes
L. A. Abbot
L. T. Meade

L. Frank Baum
Latta Griswold
Laura Dent Crane
Laura Lee Hope
Laurence Housman
Lawrence Beasley
Leo Tolstoy
Leonid Andreyev
Lewis Carroll
Lewis Sperry Chafer
Lilian Bell
Lloyd Osbourne
Louis Hughes
Louis Joseph Vance
Louis Tracy
Louisa May Alcott
Lucy Fitch Perkins
Lucy Maud Montgomery
Luther Benson
Lydia Miller Middleton
Lyndon Orr
M. Corvus
M. H. Adams
Margaret E. Sangster
Margret Howth
Margaret Vandercook
Margaret W. Hungerford
Margret Penrose
Maria Edgeworth
Maria Thompson Daviess
Mariano Azuela
Marion Polk Angellotti
Mark Overton
Mark Twain
Mary Austin
Mary Catherine Crowley
Mary Cole
Mary Hastings Bradley
Mary Roberts Rinehart
Mary Rowlandson
M. Wollstonecraft Shelley
Maud Lindsay
Max Beerbohm
Myra Kelly
Nathaniel Hawthrone
Nicolo Machiavelli
O. F. Walton
Oscar Wilde
Owen Johnson
P.G. Wodehouse
Paul and Mabel Thorne

Paul G. Tomlinson
Paul Severing
Percy Brebner
Percy Keese Fitzhugh
Peter B. Kyne
Plato
Quincy Allen
R. Derby Holmes
R. L. Stevenson
R. S. Ball
Rabindranath Tagore
Rahul Alvares
Ralph Bonehill
Ralph Henry Barbour
Ralph Victor
Ralph Waldo Emmerson
Rene Descartes
Ray Cummings
Rex Beach
Rex E. Beach
Richard Harding Davis
Richard Jefferies
Richard Le Gallienne
Robert Barr
Robert Frost
Robert Gordon Anderson
Robert L. Drake
Robert Lansing
Robert Lynd
Robert Michael Ballantyne
Robert W. Chambers
Rosa Nouchette Carey
Rudyard Kipling
Saint Augustine
Samuel B. Allison
Samuel Hopkins Adams
Sarah Bernhardt
Sarah C. Hallowell
Selma Lagerlof
Sherwood Anderson
Sigmund Freud
Standish O'Grady
Stanley Weyman
Stella Benson
Stella M. Francis
Stephen Crane
Stewart Edward White
Stijn Streuvels
Swami Abhedananda
Swami Parmananda
T. S. Ackland

T. S. Arthur
The Princess Der Ling
Thomas A. Janvier
Thomas A Kempis
Thomas Anderton
Thomas Bailey Aldrich
Thomas Bulfinch
Thomas De Quincey
Thomas Dixon
Thomas H. Huxley
Thomas Hardy
Thomas More
Thornton W. Burgess
U. S. Grant
Upton Sinclair
Valentine Williams
Various Authors
Vaughan Kester
Victor Appleton
Victor G. Durham
Victoria Cross
Virginia Woolf
Wadsworth Camp
Walter Camp
Walter Scott
Washington Irving
Wilbur Lawton
Wilkie Collins
Willa Cather
Willard F. Baker
William Dean Howells
William le Queux
W. Makepeace Thackeray
William W. Walter
William Shakespeare
Winston Churchill
Yei Theodora Ozaki
Yogi Ramacharaka
Young E. Allison
Zane Grey